The Bunko Book

The Definitive Guide to Bunko Rules, Variants, Options and Game Play

Steven Pratt

The Bunko Book

ISBN 978-0-9798362-0-6

To the women I love:
Tricia, who I chose to love
Mom, who was the first I loved
Jensen, who we all love

Acknowledgments

Thanks to the staff at the Frisco Public Library, who put up with endless search requests from me, while investigating the history of this elusive game. To David G. Schwartz, Director of the Center for Gaming Research at UNLV, who took the time to delve into the richest repository of gaming materials and confirm my earliest finds. To the tens-of-thousands of Bunko players who took the time to fill out the survey at BuncoRules.com so that we could, for the first time, really compile a substantial body of work as to how this game is played. Thanks goes to John Jones, who was forced to listen to me discuss the book on three separate 1000-mile car journeys, and encouraged me to get it done. To my niece Melissa, and her family, who put up with my badgering and submitted to being my hand model for "The Ugly Side." To the kind folks at Proctor & Gamble who allowed me unfettered access to the 2007 Bunco World Championships, and Heather Dreiling at Zoo Productions who got me in the door, when it was already completely full. To Leslie Crouch who took the time to discuss with me the history of Bunko, and the establishment of the *World Bunco Association*.

Finally, thanks to my wife and family, who encouraged me throughout the four years it took this book to go from an idea, to the finished product you now hold in your hands.

A Note on Conventions Used

When writing **The Bunko Book**, I had to work with two possible ambiguities. Do I write the name of the game as Bunco, Bunko, Bonco, or some other popular derivation? "Bunco" is the most popular, used by around 60 percent of survey respondents, but I first learned the game as Bunko, and for purely personal reasons, (and to differentiate the game from the term "Bunco" used as a swindle or cheat) I decided to use that version throughout this book. Interesting statistical facts like these will also show up sprinkled throughout the book as "Bunko Facts".

> **Bunko Fact -** *Bunko, Bunco or Bonko?*
> **58%** of groups call their game **Bunco**
> **32%** of groups call their game **Bunko**
> **6%** of groups call their game **Bonko**
> **4%** of groups are really confused!

In addition, there is always the question of personal pronouns. I have chosen to refer to players as female throughout. Since my survey indicates more than 92% of players are female, I feel justified in making this decision. Any guys reading this book – this is not a personal sleight; we are just badly outnumbered, sorry!

"I shall never believe that God plays dice with the world."

Albert Einstein

Table of Contents

What is Bunko / Bunco / Bonko?

bun·ko also bun·co (bung' ko)
n. Al. bun·kos, also bun·cos
1. A swindle in which an unsuspecting person is cheated; a confidence game.
2. A parlor game played in teams with three dice.
3. A winning throw in the above game, achieved by throwing three of a kind of a specified number.

[Probably alteration of Spanish banca, card game, from Italian banca. bank. of Germanic origin.].

Tracing the Roots

When my wife first asked me about Bunko, about six years ago, I knew almost nothing of the game. I knew my mother, an Air Force wife, had played the game, but I'd never stuck around to find out how, or why.

At my wife's prompting, I started researching the rules for her new group, and the amount of information I could find publicly was minimal to say the least. I did find two internet sites back then, Dave Holloway's Bunko site had the most information available, and the larger site, www.BuncoGame.com, which eventually rebranded and became www.DiceGamers.com, had rules, Bunko accessories, and a pretty active forum. I found a couple of other resources that had some limited information about the game, and immediately I had a problem.

Was the game Bunko (as I had learned), or Bunco? Or maybe even Bonko? Was the point 21 or 23? Did you change the number each round? What happened when you rolled all ones? All the rules were different! Picking my mother's brain wasn't very much help; she could not remember too well, and she recalled playing it different ways in different locations.

I am a curious guy. I abhor a mystery unsolved. So I did two things. First, I created www.BuncoRules.com to share what I had learned about the rules, and to create a voluntary survey, asking 24 questions about how people played the game, while including an open comments area, which provided some of the most interesting information. I didn't count on the thousands of emails I would receive!

Second, I started asking anyone and everyone about the game. I was traveling a lot, American Airlines Platinum, and on the road about half the time. Everywhere I went I asked about the game. I was astounded to find more than half the women I spoke to were familiar with the game, and almost 1 in 5 had played the game at one time or another. Men, on the other hand, knew very little of the game, and within a month or two I stopped even asking them.

Three years later, and with about 30,000 survey responses, I had learned all I could (or so I thought.) I'd read *The Sisterhood of Bunko*, and was delighted to find the author's numbers and conclusions about game play closely paralleled mine, even though her survey sample was only about a 100 respondents. I hunted down a variety of boxed versions of the game, and researched publications (to little avail) at the library and online. I had responded to thousands of emails about game play, versions of the rules, and suggestions. Strangely enough, the history of the game was still a mystery to me, and although I had read and heard a variety of reports of its origins, I still was not able to find the same information. Therefore, it was time for more research.

Earliest Accounts

The origin of the game of Bunko as played today is shrouded in mystery. There are reports that indicate women in this country played a party game of dice of some kind over a hundred years ago. The exact nature of this game is unknown; no rules for the earliest version of this game have been found. Popular in German immigrant communities at the turn of the century, it was clearly a social event, using a dice game at the center of the action, very similar to how the game is played to this day. *The Sisterhood of Bunco*[1] proposes the game was brought over from Germany.

During the 18th century, a game called 8-Dice Cloth was played in England, using three dice and having a common point scoring mechanism[2]. In the 19th century in the U.S., a game called Buck-Dice was a popular gambling game in the rough mining and logging camps. It also was based on three dice, and trying to reach a point total by rolling a specified number[3]. Leslie Crouch, the author of *It's Bunco Time!*, and founder of the World Bunco Association dates it back to this time.

What we do know for certain was sometime around the end of the 19th century there were two different games of Bunko being played in this country. One was likely a variation on Buck-Dice, and was played in illegal gambling establishments. To muddy the water, there was also a Spanish card game, Banca, being played in these gambling halls. These locations came to be known as Bunko parlors, and the unfortunate fact that many of the proprietors ran less than 100% honest games led to the use of the word bunco as a general term that applied to all swindling and confidence games.

In the meantime, in the parlors of homes, at school halls after hours, and even at some churches, women were gathering to roll dice, exchange recipes, and talk about their kids, their men, the latest in fashion and town news.

Flourishing at the Turn of the Century

After the civil war and into the turn of the century, Bunko flourished as the economy recovered, the population grew and the westward expansion took hold. During the 1880's and into the mid 1890's Bunko was played throughout the heart of the country, from Texas northward, in towns and cities along the Ohio and Mississippi rivers, and from the St. Lawrence seaway to the Great Lake states.[4] The game found itself firmly ensconced in the lives of families throughout the country, bringing one night of carefree fun into untold thousands of lives once a month.

In 1904, a different "Bunko" game was becoming popular, confusing our history even more. "Bunco" was a card game, using custom cards, which was patented in 1904 and immediately became popular. It was listed in *Hoyle's Standard Games* in 1908, and remained in this standard rules book for many years[5]. At this point Bunko was taking on many meanings. The swindle or "bunco", particularly in real-estate, the "cheating" as in the Bunco-games used on countless unsuspecting marks, the Bunco card game, which was patterned after the typical street bunco, with police cards and bunco-artist cards. And of course the seedlings of the quiet game played in communities throughout the new country, where swindling, we hope, was kept to a minimum.

Bunco Card Game – From the Pratt Bunko Collection

Prohibition and the Bunko Squad

During prohibition and the roaring 20's, the infamous Bunko gambling parlors resurfaced in various regions of the U.S. Chicago was a hotbed of Bunko Parlors, speak-easies and other locales dedicated to gambling, and drinking. The term "Bunco Squad" referred to the detectives who raided these establishments! Bunco became a common part of the language at this time, and was immortalized in movies and books about gangsters, G-men, and private detectives.

At the same time as the police were busting up Bunco Parlors, the population in this country was expanding out of the cities, creating the modern phenomenon of suburbs. The new suburbanites brought the game with them, and it finally found its true home.

While Bunko play in the heart of the city was declining during this time, it was growing in the outskirts of the city at a blistering pace!

In 1924, the dice game "Bunco" was first listed in *Hoyle's Standard Games, 4th edition.*[6] From my extensive research, including the comprehensive Taxe Library of Gambling and the Library of Congress, this is the first official rules of the game I could unearth. This game is essentially the same game as played today, with three dice being rolled, a "progressive" trump required to score points, and a score of 23 required to win a round.

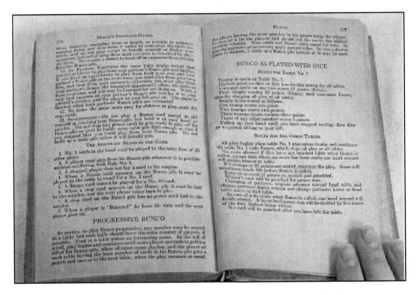

Bunco Entry in Hoyle's Standard Rules, 4ᵗʰ Edition

Somehow, going into World War II, evidence of the game becomes sparse, and apparently, its play declined during this time of transition in this country, not to resurface, in earnest, for nearly 40 years.

The post war years were not kind to the game of Bunko, yet it was tenaciously kept alive in small pockets throughout the country. It was in the 1980's that it started its remarkable comeback, with grown women starting up groups based on their memory of games played by their parents and neighbors decades earlier.

Commercial attempts to revive the game also came into being with several boxed (and trademarked) versions of the game springing into being. Its revival was still tentative, and slow going and most of these efforts failed, at first. In the 1990's this revival continued, and the World Bunko Association was formed around 1997, to help further the game and standardize rules.

Bunko Today

A desire for a return to traditional family values, a sense of neighborhood and community and the desire and need for social interaction has fueled the fire of Bunko, and it is experiencing a growth that is nothing less than phenomenal. Still primarily found in suburban communities, it is expanding into college campuses, summer camps and retreats, fellowship groups, and community events. The US Military has helped the growth enormously; Bunko has long been a favorite with Army/Navy/Air Force wives, and as they traveled to their new posts, they brought the game with them. Whereas 20 years ago, there may have been a few hundred thousand people playing Bunko around the country, conservative estimates put the number of regular Bunko players today at over seven million![7]

Although primarily an American game, it has certainly crossed the northern border in large numbers. It has been spotted in over 80 countries. During the research for this book, I have personally met with, talked to and occasionally sat in on Bunko groups from England, Sweden, Spain, Panama, Israel, Hawaii, and even Beijing, China.

Traditionally most Bunko groups consist of 12 players (usually groups of women & occasionally couples.) Kids are even beginning to play at parties and other social events. Playing Bunko is a great way to maintain relationships and make new friends.

Today Bunko is commonly considered a woman's game, with neighborhood Bunko groups popping up everywhere. In the center of the country, it seems every new home development is accompanied by a flyer advertising the formation of a new Bunko group. Some realtors and housing developers even advertise the presence of Bunko groups to indicate a dynamic and social community.

In 2006, we even had the first **World Bunco Championships**. More than a thousand women and men from all around the country migrated to Las Vegas for the weekend, to attend the Prilosec™ OTC sponsored event, giving away a Grand Prize of $50,000! This event was so popular that the following year, several regionals were held to win places at the World Championships, and open registration was filled within hours of opening, after selling out. Lifetime Channel™ even made a TV show of the event, tracking the progress of several individuals throughout the tournament.

Bunko FACT - Bunko has been around a while - during our research for this book, we found over a hundred women who've been playing for at least 40 years, and more than two dozen with over 50 years of game play under their belt. That's a lot of Bunkos!

Official Bunko / Bunco?

Bunko's grass roots origins and word-of-mouth existence have led to an unusual element. The rules of Bunko are as varied as the people who play it. Wherever you find people playing Bunko, you can find a slightly different version of the game. There is a core set of rules that are essential to the game, and the vast majority of all games have these elements in common.

There are several "official" versions of the game available, and numerous trademarks have been filed for variations of the game.

The earliest boxed Bunko game I have came from the Ungame Company back in 1988. *Bunco Deluxe* was a full sized game, with bell, dice, scorecards and simple rules.

Bunco Deluxe – From the Pratt Bunko Collection

www.Bunco.com sells the *Bunco® Dice Game*, and has had a trademark on the name Bunco for parlor games since 1992.

Bunco Dice Game – From the Pratt Bunko Collection

A trademark was registered in 1999 for "periodicals, namely newsletters, magazines, books, and booklets in the field of travel, cooking, parlor games, and parlor game tournaments, and calendars". The owner went on to further trademark a very popular boxed version of the game called *It's Bunco Time!!!®*, available at the website www.eBunco.com. They also registered The World Bunco Association® around the same time, "dedicated to the organization, preservation, promotion and the expansion of Bunco group activity." The World Bunco Association works with Proctor and Gamble's *Prilosec OTC*, to sponsor the World Bunco Championship®.

It's Bunco Time!!! – From the Pratt Bunko Collection

Another version of the game has been out for several years: *The Box of Bunco®*. This version of the game was trademarked in 2002, but the trademark was abandoned in 2004. It is still commonly found at many online retailers.

You only have to visit eBay to find numerous versions of the game out there for sale. Fundex games carries the *Bunco Party™ Game,* which can be found on several websites, and is carried in many retail stores such as Target and Toys-R-Us.

Girls' Night Out is a beautifully boxed Bunko game, whose subtitle "a Bunko Dice Game," is right up our alley. Made by CR Gibson, they have recently updated their look and the new version of their game includes a "traveling" tiara.

Girl's Night Out – From the Pratt Bunko Collection

Hallmark released the *Barbie Bunko & Game Set*™ to celebrate Barbie's 45th Anniversary. A really cute hat-box version of the game which also included cards, and one of the few published games out there to call themselves a "Bunko" game.

Southern Living at Home also sold a "Bunco" game, that came in a very nice wooden box, ideal for passing the materials from one player to the next, between game nights.

There's even an I Love Lucy Bunco game that comes in a party purse.

Many, many more versions of the game exist, including free versions given away with Frangelica liquor, and even online games.

Southern Living at Home Bunko – Pratt Bunko Collection

As one might guess, there were some drastically different versions of rules produced with these games.

So what are the official rules of the game? It is not for us to judge, but the rules posted by the World Bunco Association are some of the closest to the core rule set that I find most people to be playing by traditionally, and as the rules provider for the World Bunco Championship, I have seen them work for thousands of players from all over the country. On the other hand, if you based your game on the 1924 version of the game printed in *Hoyle's Standard Games*, you would certainly have history working on your side.

I still like what they say over at Bunco Central, www.BuncoCentral.com, "different groups around the country each have their own style of play and their own set of Bunko rules. So feel free to tweak the rules. Just make sure you're consistent."

In *The Bunko Book,* I have gathered the rules of the game from a variety of printed sources, from internet resources, and through surveys and interviews with tens of thousands of players. You are holding the results of my analysis in your hands. With this book in hand, you are in a great position to make the game your own.

---

[1] Maite G. Franck, The Sisterhood of Bunco: A Comprehensive Guide to the Game, (Santa Maria, CA: Bittersweet Press, 1997) 112.

[2] Leslie Crouch, It's Bunco Time! Cookbook and Party Ideas, (Hyperion, 2004) 123

[3] John Scarne, Scarne on Dice, (Harrisburg: Military Service Publishing Co, 1945) 422

[4] Crouch, 114

[5] Hoyle's Standard Games, (Chicago: Laird & Lee, 1908) 349

[6] Hoyle's Standard Games, (Chicago: Laird & Lee, 1924) 238

[7] www.prnewswire.com (Proctor & Gamble, 3/23/2007)

"One who doesn't throw the dice can
never expect to score a six."
Navjot Singh Sidhu

As I have discussed Bunko has many variations in play, and in organization. None of the rules is written in stone, and it is up to your group to decide how they want to play the game. In order to explain the game I am going to start with the most basic play style, and the most common group organization.

The rules of the game are relatively easy to learn and understand, it's the execution of the rules that causes much of the difficulties

---

Bunko FACT – According to my survey, **86%** of regular Bunko players play in groups of **12**. About **5%** play in groups of **8**, **6%** in groups of **16**, and the remaining **3%** in all KINDS of odd combinations.

Bunko is a game of dice, played in rounds and sets. Players take turns rolling the dice and trying to accumulate points in order to win each "round" at their table.

Bunko is played with three dice. All three are rolled at the same time. Points are accumulated by rolling the "Mark". The Mark may be fixed (six is common), or may change each round or set.

Players continue rolling as long as they score at least 1 point on their roll. If they fail to score a point, the game continues clockwise, with the person to their left collecting the dice and getting their chance to score.

Play is controlled from the Head Table. Once a team at the Head Table scores enough points to win, they announce the end of the round, and the team with the highest score at each lower table wins the round.

Game Play (EZ-Bunko)

EZ-Bunko is a simplified version of the game, and well suited to games where you may have new players, such as with new groups and fundraisers. The game is played at three tables of four players in competing teams of two. Partners sit opposite each other, and keep score for each other while the other is rolling.

Each player rolls a die to see who goes first. Play then rotates from player to player clockwise after a player fails to score.

The tables are "ranked". There is a Head Table, a Low Table, and a Middle Table. When your team wins a game, it advances to the next higher table, leaving the losers to stay at the same table. At the Head Table, the winners remain and the losers go to the Low Table.

You change partners after each round, including at the Head Table. Players at each table who remain behind decide who will change seats. When the advancing team sits down, they are no longer partnered. This might seem a little confusing now, but in the game play section, I will walk you through a round.

The Head Table controls play. Play starts with an announcement from the Head Table (commonly by using a bell.) During each round, the teams at the Head Table try to score 21 points or more.

Points are scored as follows:

- ⊡ One Mark scores one point.
- ⊡ Two Marks score two points.
- ⊡ Three Marks score twenty-one points. (Bunko)
- ⊡ Three of any other number scores five points.

The first team to score 21 points at the Head Table wins the round and calls out a stop to play, again, usually with a bell. At all other tables play stops when the Head Table play stops and the team with the highest score at each lower table win the round. If there is a tie at a table when play stops, play continues normally until the tie is broken. In addition, every person at the lower table is entitled to roll the dice at least once. Therefore, if the Head Table scores a Bunko very quickly, the other tables can continue to roll until each person has had at least one roll.

Note that scoring is separate at each table. Winning scores at the lower tables could be 1 or 50 (or more!), depending on the rolling. However, a winning score is the higher score and will always be at least 21 at the Head Table.

At this point, play in this round is complete. Winners mark their wins on their scoring sheets, and losers mark their losses.

During play, players track the number of rounds they win and lose as a team, and the number of Bunkos scored individually, on their personal scorecard.

At the end of the night wins/losses and Bunkos are tallied and prizes awarded. Ties are broken by dice roll.

Money is the prize most commonly played for. Each player kicks in a set amount - $10 for example, for a total prize pool of $120. The prize money is divided up at the end of play according to the house rules. Example prize rules are provided at the end of the game rules.

Game Vocabulary

The game of Bunko has a game play vocabulary associated with it that is pretty simple and easy to remember. The key terms of play are:

Break: The essential time between sets, when appetizers, entrees and desserts are served, and bladders are emptied.

Bunko: Rolling three of a kind of the Mark or point you were trying to roll, usually worth 21 points.

Baby-Bunko (or *Baby*, *Monte-Carlo*, *Overs*, etc.): Three of a kind of any number other than the mark. A Baby-Bunko usually scores 5 points, and allows the turn to continue.

Bunko Babe: The most popular reference for a player of Bunko.

Ghost: The stand-in for a missing player when there are less than 12 people playing. Most groups have some item that represents the "ghost" player.

Head Table: The game tables in Bunko are not all equal. The Head Table is the winner's table and controls the play. During the game, players advance to the Head Table by winning rounds.

Hostess: She who hosts the Bunko Party. The Maker of rules, provider of eats, and overall game dictator for a day.

Mark (or *Point*): The number you are trying to roll each round. Also sometimes referred to as the Point or Trump.

Pot: Accumulated cash prize. Most Bunko groups play for cash or prizes. You put your $$ for the night into the pot which is split at the end of the night according to game rules.

Round: One turn of play, where teams try to score points by rolling a certain number.

Set: Six rounds. Bunko is played in sets. Between sets is a great time for snacks and drinks.

Traveling: Passing an item around during play to indicate an event, usually the last player to score Bunko.

Wipeout: A popular option where rolling a certain number (such as three ones) wipes out a team's current score and ends the turn.

EZ-Bunko

The Official Ten Rules of EZ-Bunko - the simplest form of the game.

Materials:
- 12 players
- 3 Tables
- 3 dice per table
- 1 pad of scratch-paper per table
- 1 pencil per table
- 1 score-card per person
- 1 Bell

Rule 1: Score Points by Rolling Three Dice

The object of the game of EZ-Bunko is to win rounds of play by out scoring your opponents. The Mark in EZ-Bunko is always six. A player scores by rolling sixes on any of their three dice when thrown. Players may also score by rolling three of a kind of any other number. A player continues rolling as long as they score one or more points per throw. Point scoring is as follows:

     1 die showing a six = 1 point.
     2 dice (or doubles) showing sixes = 2 points
     3 dice showing sixes = 21 points
     3 of a kind dice of any other number = 5 points

Rule 2: Legal Rolls

In order for a roll to count, the dice must be lifted off the table, shaken and rolled onto the table. Dice scores count only if the dice land cleanly. If the dice land stacked or cocked all three dice are re-rolled. If any of the dice fall on the floor, all three dice are re-rolled. If one or more dice fall off the table twice during any one players turn, that ends their turn.

Rule 3: Ranking Tables and Teams

One table is designated the Head Table and controls the pace of play. The other tables are assigned an arbitrary order from lowest to highest.

Rule 4: Initial Setup

Players roll three dice for initial table selection. The highest four rolls sit at the Head Table, the next four highest at the Middle Table, and so on. Players choose their seat at random initially. Dice are rolled at each table to determine who rolls first.

Rule 5: Keeping Score

The rolling player's partner is the scorekeeper and is tasked with keeping score on scratch paper. There is no specific manner in which this scoring should be kept. Scorekeepers may use scratch paper, or at the discretion of the group, mechanical counters, or any other device they may deem appropriate. At the end of each player's roll, the scorekeeper adds the player's score to the running total for their team, and announces the new team score. Any player who rolls a Bunko should mark the result on her personal score-card.

Rule 6: Playing the Round

At the start of each round, the last player to roll from the team remaining at the table from the previous round starts the next round. The round begins with a signal from the Head Table by ringing the bell, and the players at each table begin the rolling. A round is completed when one of the teams at the Head Table scores at least 21 points. The current scorekeeper announces the end of the round again by ringing the bell, and the turns end at all tables. No score is allowed if the dice have not touched the table when the end of the round has been called, with the exception that all players are entitled to roll at least once.

Rule 7: Tracking Wins and Losses

When either team at the Head Table scores 21 they have won the round. At the lower tables, whichever team has the most points when the rolling is ended, wins the round. If there is a tie at one of the lower tables, play continues as normal until one of the teams score and break the tie. After all rolling has been completed, each player from the winning team should tally a win on her personal scorecard for that round. Each player from the losing team should tally a loss on her personal scorecard. Tallies may be marked any way as is deemed appropriate and agreed upon.

Rule 8: Advancing Tables

When all scores have been updated players change places and teams. Players from the winning team at the lower tables advance one table rank towards the Head Table. The losing players at all the lower tables remain at their table, the last person to roll at the table switching seats. The losers from the Head table move to the lowest table. No one should play with the same partner twice in a row.

Rule 9: End of the Game

The players should decide ahead of time when the game will end. This may be at a selected number of Sets (3 or 4 is common) or at a predetermined time. When the game is over, players compute their total wins, losses and Bunkos, and prizes are awarded based on overall results.

Rule 10: Distributing Prizes

At the end of the night, any ties between players for prizes are determined by individual roll offs. Each player in the tie gets a turn rolling for a six, and accumulates points until they fail to score (as in regular play). The player with the highest score wins the tiebreaker. Players continue taking turns rolling until there is no longer a tie. Players may win more than 1 prize.

Prizes ($120 pool - $10 per person):
- ⊡ Most Wins - person with most **W** (Wins) ($50)
- ⊡ Most Bunkos - person with most Bunkos rolled ($30)
- ⊡ Most Losses – person with most **L** (Losses) ($20)
- ⊡ Consolation ($10) - Random drawing from all non-winners

> "Roll me and call me the tumblin'
> dice."
> *Rolling Stones*

Progressive Bunko is a lot like EZ-Bunko, and is the most common version of the game being played today. I consider this the standard version of Bunko, and any reference to the game Bunko will refer to Progressive Bunko unless otherwise noted. In Progressive Bunko, the "Mark" that the players try to roll in order to score points changes each round. Each "Set" has six rounds, and the Mark to roll corresponds to the number of the current round. In the first round, everyone tries to roll ones. In the second round, twos, and so on. Again, rolling the Mark on all three dice is still called a Bunko, and rolling three of anything else is called a Baby-Bunko (or Baby).

At the beginning of each new Set, the Mark is reset to one, and the round number starts at one as well.

Bunko FACT – On your mark, get set…

82% of Bunko games use the round # as the mark.
9% use the number 6.
5% use the number 5 or 4
Less than **1%** use the number 2.
Less than 1/10 of **1%** use the number 3
Only 3 people confessed to using the 1 as the Mark!

Progressive Bunko

The Official Twelve Rules of Progressive Bunko - the most common form of the game.

Materials:
- ▣ At least 8 players, 12 players are recommended.
- ▣ 1 table per 4 people
- ▣ 3 dice per table
- ▣ 1 or more scratch-pads per table
- ▣ 1 or more pencils per table
- ▣ 1 score card per person
- ▣ 1 Bell at the Head Table (for starting and stopping rounds)
- ▣ 1 soft, tossable item (Fuzzy Die, stuffed animal, etc.)

Rule 1: Score Points by Rolling Three Dice

The object of the game of Bunko is to win rounds of play by out scoring your opponents. Players score by rolling three dice and matching the current number or Mark, which has been established for that round. Players take turns rolling the dice. A player continues rolling as long as they score one or more points per throw. Point scoring is as follows (example is for Round 2, making the Mark 2):

⚁⚁⚁ 1 die showing the Mark = 1 point.

⚁⚁⚀ 2 dice (or doubles) showing the Mark = 2 points

⚁⚁⚁ 3 dice showing the current Mark = 21 points

⚂⚂⚂ 3 of a kind of any other number = 5 points

Rule 2: Legal Rolls

In order for a roll to count, the dice must be lifted off the table, shaken and rolled on the table. Dice scores count only if the dice land cleanly. If the dice land stacked or cocked all three dice are re-rolled. If any of the dice fall on the floor, all three dice are re-rolled. If the dice fall off the table twice during one player's turn, that ends their turn.

Rule 3: Ranking Tables and Teams

One table is designated the Head Table. The Head Table controls the pace of play. The other tables are assigned an arbitrary order from lowest to highest.

Rule 4: Initial Setup

Players roll 3 dice for initial table selection. The highest four rolls sit at the Head Table, the next four highest at the second highest table, and so on. Players choose their seat at random initially. Dice are rolled at each table to determine who rolls first. The Hostess starts with possession of the Traveler token.

Rule 5: Keeping Score

The rolling player's partner is the scorekeeper and is tasked with keeping score during the rolling. There is no specific manner in which this scoring should be kept. Scorekeepers may use scratch paper, mechanical counters, or any other device they may deem appropriate. At the end of each player's roll, the scorekeeper adds the player's score to the running total for their team, and announces the new team score. Any player who rolls a Bunko should mark the result on her personal scorecard.

Rule 6: Establishing the Mark

Progressive Bunko is played in Sets, which consist of 6 rounds. The Mark (point to be rolled) for each round is established at the beginning of that round, and is announced by the initial scorekeeper at the Head Table. The Mark starts at one and advances by one up to six, matching the number of the round within the set. E.g. Round one, the Mark is 1. Round two, the Mark is 2, and so on up to Round six, where the Mark is 6. Announcing the Mark is a courtesy and no penalty is incurred if the scorekeeper fails to announce the Mark.

Rule 7: "Traveling"

Bunko is played with a 'Traveling' token, commonly a stuffed animal or fuzzy die, called the "Traveler". When a player rolls a Bunko (three of the Mark), the current keeper of the Traveler throws it at whoever rolled the Bunko. At the end of game play, the person who has the Traveler wins a separate prize. Any rolling of a Bunko, including rolling at a lower table after the Head Table has announced the end of the game, such as a roll-off, is valid for exchange of the Traveler.

Rule 8: Playing the Round

At the start of each round, the last player to roll from the team remaining at the table from the previous round starts the next round. The round begins with a signal from the scorekeeper at the Head Table, usually by ringing the bell, and the players at each table begin the rolling. A round is completed when one of the teams at the Head Table scores 21 or more points. The current scorekeeper announces the end of the round again by ringing the bell, and the turns end at all tables. No score is allowed if the dice have not touched the table when the end of the round has been called, with the exception that all players are entitled to roll at least once.

Rule 9: Tracking Wins and Losses

When either team at the Head Table scores 21 they have won the round. At the lower tables, whichever team has the most points when the rolling is ended, wins the round. If there is a tie at one of the lower tables, play continues as normal until one of the teams score and break the tie. After all rolling has been completed, each player from the winning team should tally a win on her personal scorecard for that round. Players from the losing team should tally a loss on their personal scorecard. Tallies may be marked any way deemed appropriate.

Rule 10: Advancing Tables

When all scores have been updated players change places and teams. Players from the winning team at the lower tables advance one table rank towards the Head Table. The losing players at all the lower tables remain at their table, the last person to roll at the table switching seats with an open one. The losers from the Head table move to the lowest table. No one should play with the same partner twice in a row.

Rule 11: End of the Game

The players should decide ahead of time when the game will end. This may be at a selected number of Sets (3 or 4 is common) or at a predetermined time. When the game is over, players compute their total wins, losses and Bunkos, and prizes are awarded based on overall results.

Rule 12: Distributing Prizes

At the end of the night, any ties between players for prizes are determined by individual roll offs. Each player in the tie gets a turn rolling for a six, and accumulates points until they fail to score (as in regular play). The player with the highest score wins the tiebreaker. Players continue taking turns rolling until there is no longer a tie. Players may win more than 1 prize.

Prizes ($120 pool - $10 per person)
- Most Wins - person with most **W** (Wins) ($50)
- Most Bunkos ($30)
- Traveling - Last person to roll Bunko ($20)
- Most Losses – person with most **L** (Losses) ($10)
- Consolation prize – selected randomly from everyone who didn't win a prize ($10)

```
         "Somebody breathin' down my neck
        While I'm tryin' to roll the bones
        I don't care I'll just float a check
        Cause I'm feelin' my gamblin' Jones"
                     ZZ Top
```

A sample round

To see how the game is played, let's follow the action for one round as played at all three of the tables. The game played is Progressive Bunko using the standard rules including changing the Mark each round, and using a 'Traveler'.

Action at the Head Table – Alice, Brenda, Charlotte and Debbie

The players have rolled their dice to see who goes first, and Alice has rolled an eleven on two dice, winning the right to start. Her partner, Charlotte, sitting across from her, becomes the scorekeeper.

The scorekeeper (Charlotte) at the Head Table announces that the Mark is one and rings the bell to indicate start of play. Play begins at all tables.

▢⚀⚁ **Alice** rolls 145 – Scores 1 point and gets to roll again. The scorekeeper (Charlotte) tallies a 1 under "US" on the scratchpad.

⚂⚂⚁ **Alice** rolls 334 – Scores 0 points. The dice pass to Brenda on her left, but Alice does not handle the dice after she fails to score, in order not to slow down Brenda. Charlotte passes the scratchpad to Debbie, on her left.

⚂⚄⚅ **Brenda** shakes the dice and rolls 356 – Scores 0 points and gives up the dice. Debbie tallies a 0 for "THEM". The scratchpad is passed to Alice.

BUNKO Table Tally	
Us	**Them**
1	0

⚀⚀⚁ **Charlotte**, Alice's partner, quickly scoops up the dice and rolls 112. She scores 2 points and gets to roll again. Alice marks 2 more points on the scratchpad.

⚃⚃⚃ **Charlotte** rolls 444 – Announces "Baby", scores 5 points, which is recorded by Alice, and rolls again.

⚁⚂⚄ **Charlotte rolls** 235 – Scores 0 points. The dice pass to Debbie on her left. Alice announces her teams score, 8, and passes the scratchpad to Brenda.

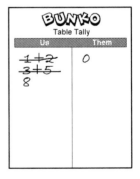

BUNKO Table Tally	
Us	**Them**
~~1 + 2~~ ~~3 + 5~~ 8	0

⚄⚄⚄ **Debbie** rolls 555 – Scores 5 points, tallied by Brenda, and gets to roll again.

⊡⊡⊡ **Debbie** rolls 111 – She shouts Bunko! Since she is seated at the Head Table, Brenda rings the table bell, indicating end of play. While Debbie marks a 'B' on her scorecard for her Bunko, she is hit in the head by a large Fuzzy Traveling die.

Alice and her partner Charlotte mark 'L's on their scorecard and move to the Low Table. Debbie and Brenda mark 'W's on their scorecard. Debbie as the last player to roll moves one seat to her left and will get to start the rolling when the next round starts.

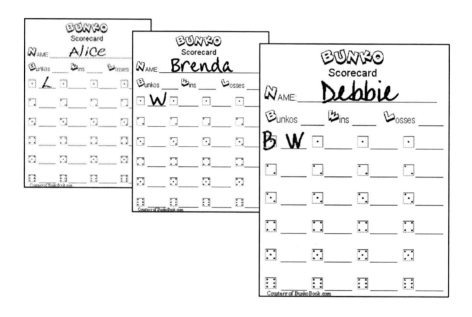

Action at the Middle Table - Anne, Betty, Candi, and Donna

The scorekeeper at the Head Table announced that the Mark is one and rang the bell to indicate start of play. Anne won the roll-off and takes control of the dice. Her partner Candi takes the scratchpad as the initial scorekeeper.

▢▢▢ Anne rolls 113 – Scores 2 points and gets to roll again

▢▢▢ Anne rolls 334 – Scores 0 points. Candi tallies 2 point for "US" and passes the scorecard to Donna on her left.

▢▢▢ Betty who now has the dice rolls 144 – Scores 1 point and rolls again

▢▢▢ Betty rolls 344 – Scoring 0 points. Donna, her partner, tallies a 1 under "THEM" the passes the scratchpad.

▢▢▢ Candi, Anne's partner, rolls 112 – Scores 2 points and gets to roll again.

▢▢▢ Candi rolls 255 – Scores 0 points and the dice pass to her left. Anne crosses out the 2 (previous team score), adds 2 (the points that Candi scored), and writes down the new score, 4, before passing the scratchpad to Betty.

▢▢▢ Donna rolls 111 – And shouts **Bunko** scoring 21 points. Donna marks a B on her scorecard for her Bunko, and is pelted with the large Fuzzy Traveling die by Asia, our hostess, at the Low Table, who is the custodian of the Traveler at the beginning of the game.

▢▢▢ Donna rolls 566 – Scores 0 points and passes the dice to her left. Betty crosses out the 1 (previous team score), adds 21 (the points that Donna scored), and writes down the new score for "THEM" - 22.

BUNKO Table Tally	
Us	Them
✗ 4	✗ 22

▢▢▢ Anne rolls: 333 – Announces "Baby" and scores 5 points and rolls again.

The game bell rings at the Head Table where Debbie shouts BUNKO, indicating the end of play. Donna throws the Traveling Die at Debbie and hits her on the head! Woohoo!!

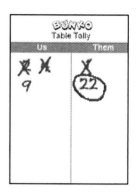

Anne's turn has been abruptly terminated. Her partner Candi tallies her final score – adds 5 points to the existing 4 points for a total of 9.

The team of Betty and Donna win the round, having scored 22 to Anne and Candi's score of 9.

Anne and her partner Candi mark 'L's on their scorecard. Donna and Betty mark 'W's on their scorecard and move to the High Table.

Anne, as the last player to roll remaining at the table, takes the dice and moves one seat to her left. New players from the Lower Table sit wherever they want in the remaining two seats.

Action at the Low Table - Asia, Beverly, Carmen and Denise

The Scorekeeper at the Head Table announced the Mark is one and rang the bell to indicate start of play. Asia, our hostess, at the Low Table takes the dice. Her partner Carmen is the score-keeper.

⚂⚀⚂ Asia rolls: 334 – Scores 0 points. Carmen tallies 0 points for "US" and passes the scratchpad to her left.

⚀⚁⚂ Beverly who quickly claimed the dice rolls 244 – Scores 0 points and passes the dice to her left. Denise tallies 0 points for "THEM" before passing the scratchpad.

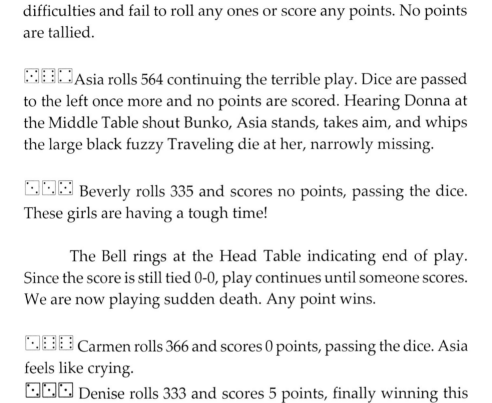

Carmen (246) and Denise (456) continue to have difficulties and fail to roll any ones or score any points. No points are tallied.

Asia rolls 564 continuing the terrible play. Dice are passed to the left once more and no points are scored. Hearing Donna at the Middle Table shout Bunko, Asia stands, takes aim, and whips the large black fuzzy Traveling die at her, narrowly missing.

Beverly rolls 335 and scores no points, passing the dice. These girls are having a tough time!

The Bell rings at the Head Table indicating end of play. Since the score is still tied 0-0, play continues until someone scores. We are now playing sudden death. Any point wins.

Carmen rolls 366 and scores 0 points, passing the dice. Asia feels like crying.

Denise rolls 333 and scores 5 points, finally winning this round and ending this debacle, in spite of the fact that none of the players EVER rolled the Mark.

The teams mark their scorecards with their wins and losses. Beverly and Denise proudly move on to the Middle Table. Carmen shifts one seat to her left, takes the dice, and hopes for a better partner this next round!

Bunko FACT:
Bunko is played by all ages. We had respondents ranging from 7 years old up to 89.
The AVERAGE age? 40 years young.

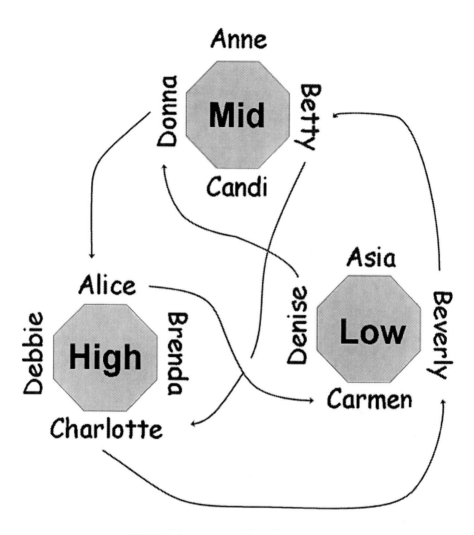

Table Movement after First Round

> "Not only does God play dice,
> he sometimes throws them where they
> cannot be seen."
> *Stephen Hawking*

When discussing the numerous different ways that Bunko is being played, the differences are referred to as Variants and Options.

Variants are deviations from the basic rules of the games, and create a slightly different form of play.

Options are game elements that can usually be brought into any game of Bunko or Bunko variant.

Bunko FACT:
96% of all groups end their games at 21 points
3% score until **23**
Only **1%** use any other way of ending the round!

Variants

Variants fall into three broad categories: establishing a Mark, scoring a round, and ending a round.

Establishing a Mark

In Bunko, the Mark or point you are trying to score matches the current Round number in that set. For example in Round 1, the Mark is 1. In Round 3, the Mark is three. Numerous variations exist in setting this mark, of which a few are listed here.

Sixes (aka BoxCars, EZ-Bunko)

In this, the most common variant, the Mark is always six, and does not change each round. Three sixes is always Bunko, and three of any other number is usually called "Baby-Bunko", "Baby", or "Overs", scoring 5 points. The scoring is the same as for standard Bunko, with one six worth 1 point, 2 sixes worth 2 points, and three sixes worth 21 points.

Onesies

A rare variant, the Mark is always one, and does not change each round. Three ones is always Bunko, and three of any other number is usually called "Baby-Bunko", "Baby", or "Overs", scoring 5 points. The scoring is the same as for standard Bunko, with a single one scoring 1 point, 2 ones worth 2 points, and three ones, a Bunko, worth 21 points.

Christian

A popular variant, this is almost exactly the opposite of Sixes. In Christian, each SET is only 5 rounds, and the Mark is incremented as in normal Bunko from 1 to 5. However, in Christian, six is never the Mark. Christian is usually combined with Wipeout (option) and rolling 3 sixes at any time causes you to lose your turn and all points scored up until that time. Even when not playing Wipeout, no points are awarded for three sixes, and the player loses the roll. Scoring is otherwise the same as standard Bunko.

Odd Mark

In this unusual variant, the Mark is a number other than 1 or 6, and doesn't change each round. Three of the odd Mark is always Bunko, and three of any other number is usually called Baby-Bunko, scoring 5 points. The scoring is the same as for standard Bunko, with one of the odd Mark worth 1 point, 2 Marks worth 2 points, and three Marks worth 21 points.

Rolled Point

This original method of scoring, as recorded in Hoyle's Standard Games, is not nearly as common today. At the beginning of each round, the first player to roll at the Head Table rolls a single die, establishing the initial Mark. That number is announced and becomes the Mark that everyone will try to roll. The Mark is then re-rolled at the beginning of each new round. A set is usually six rounds.

Confusion (aka Reset)

The Mark is constantly changing. Anyone at the Head Table rolling three of a kind that isn't a Bunko, scores 5 points and the number rolled is the new Mark. For example, during Round 2, the starting Mark is 2. While rolling, a player rolls 3 fours. They would score 5 points and the new Mark is 4 for the remainder of that round, or until a new Mark is established. The player rolling the three of a kind must loudly announce the new mark, and all tables must repeat it. Rolling 3 fours now would be a Bunko.

Scoring a Round

Normal Bunko scores points by rolling the established Mark. One die showing the Mark scores one point. Two dice with the Mark scores 2 points. Three Dice with the Mark scores 21 points, three of a kind of any other number scores 5 points. There are a huge number of variations in scoring, and I will list only some of the most common.

1,2,3 (a.k.a. Low)

In this slow playing version of the game, you only get one point each time you roll the Mark, no matter what. One Mark = 1 point. Two Marks = 2 points. Three Marks = 3 points = Bunko. Scoring a Bunko does not automatically end the round. Rolling three of any other number does not score any points, but you are allowed to keep rolling. This is usually referred to as Overs.

1,5,10

One Mark rolled gives one point. Two Marks rolled (doubles) scores 5 points. Three-of-a-kind of any number except the Mark scores 5 points. Three of a kind of the Mark, Bunko, scores 10 points. Bunko does not end game play.

Overs

Game is scored the same as regular Bunko, except that rolling three of a kind of any number other than the Mark allows the player to keep rolling, but scores no points.

Doubles

This scoring is Mark dependent. One Mark rolled gives one point. Two Marks rolled (doubles) scores double the Mark. If the Mark is 1, doubles is worth 2 points. If the Mark is 2, doubles is worth 4 points (2 doubled). Similarly, if the Mark is 3, 4, 5 or 6, doubles are worth 6, 8, 10 or 12 respectively. Three Marks rolled (Bunko) still scores 21. Three of a kind of any other number scores 5 points and continues rolling. Rolling a Bunko at the Head Table still wins the game automatically.

No BABIES

No Babies is played exactly like regular Bunko, except that rolling three of a kind of any number other than the Mark is worth nothing. No points are scored and your turn ends. It is just a wasted three of a kind.

Ending the Round

During normal Bunko, the Head Table drives the pace of play. When a team at the Head Table scores 21 points the round ends for all tables, any players at the lower tables stop rolling.

Odd Point

In an Odd Point game, the number to win a round is some number other than 21. A goal of 23 is the most common Odd Point. It is also the scoring goal listed in the earliest documented rules. Thirty (30) is another common odd point, although I'm not certain why. Whatever the odd point is, rolling a Bunko is usually worth that many points. When the Odd Point is 23, the game ends at 23 and the point total awarded for a Bunko is 23.

Bunko to Win

The Head Table continues rolling until a Bunko is rolled. Points at the Head Table are immaterial. Warning: This can make for a very long game.

Any Bunko

Every table is equipped with a bell, and anyone who rolls a Bunko stops play. Any Bunko, at any table, ends the round and stops play at all the tables.

Any Win

Every table is equipped with a bell, and anyone who rolls a Bunko or scores 21 stops play. Any win (Bunko or 21), at any table, ends the round and stops play at all the tables. This variant is sometimes played with very large groups where there are 5 or more tables playing.

Dead Stop

The point does not change, it remains 21. When the Head Table stops play after scoring 21, all play stops immediately at all tables. Any dice not ON THE TABLE, when play is stopped are not scored. Players at lower tables do not get to continue their scoring. This is the most common method of ending scoring.

Roll-on

The opposite of dead stop. When the end of the game is announced at the Head Table, players rolling at the lower tables, who have already rolled at least once, get to continue rolling until they fail to score. All players are entitled to the same number of turns rolling the dice. Their entire score is counted towards the final team total. This is the method of scoring used at the Bunko World Championships.

Options

Options are small variations in the game play added just for fun. They don't change the basic rules usually, but add twists to the game play. Options can be grouped into four different categories. These can be generalized as Scoring, Rolling, Moving and Sidebars.

Scoring

Scoring involves not only the scoring of points for rolling the current Mark, but also the tracking of Bunkos and other "special" rolls. These rolls may be the basis for prize distribution at the end of the night.

Traveling

> **Bunco FACT:** Traveling is the most common option by far. More than **87%** of all Bunko Groups incorporate Traveling in their game rules.

If you choose to add Traveling to your game, the "Fuzzy Die" or other (preferably soft, tossable) object is added. "Traveling" occurs whenever a Bunko is rolled. The current custodian of the Fuzzy Die throws the die at the person who called Bunko. The hostess usually starts with the Traveler token.

The player holding the die or object at the end of the game wins the traveler prize!

In some cases, the player who rolls the Bunko actually selects an object (prize), and the prize is passed to each person who afterwards rolls a Bunko.

Traveling and Wipeout can be played with a wide variety of items to indicate who had the last Bunko or Wipeout. When playing with themes, it is fun to match the Traveling item to the night's theme (for example, wearing a set of dice-beads for Mardi-Gras, wearing an oversized sombrero for Cinco-de-Mayo, or even a Santa hat).

Wipeout (a.k.a. Snake Eyes)

When playing Wipeout, each set is only played from 2 to 6. The ones round is skipped. During Wipeout, rolling three ones is called a Wipeout, and the person rolling the Wipeout loses all their points for the round and must start over, but they get to continue rolling the dice.

Traveling Wipeout is played like regular Traveling, but a different soft fuzzy is thrown around and whoever holds it at the end of play gets a consolation prize.

Dirty Bunko (Dirty Wipeout)

(Get your mind out of the gutter!) Dirty Bunko is the same as Wipeout, except that the player who rolls the Wipeout also loses their turn.

Weighted Scoring (aka High Scores)

With weighted scoring, the High Table uses a different color pen (typically RED) to write down 'W's for wins and 'L's for losses. The Middle and Low Tables use a blue or black pen.

At the end of play, when scores are totaled, High Table scores (red marks) count double, both as wins and losses. When totaling the score each Red 'W' would count as 2 and each Red 'L' would count as two. Blue and black 'W's and 'L's count as one point each.

Most Win points, not the most 'W's, wins. Most Loss points, not the most 'L's, wins.

Monte Carlos

Some groups keep track of 3-of-a-kinds that are not Bunkos. These are usually called "Baby-Bunkos" or "Babies" or "Monte-Carlos." Rolling a Monte-Carlo entitles the roller to write an M on their scorecard. (When using the name "Baby-Bunkos" or "Babies" players write a small "b" for Babies and a Capital "B" for Bunkos.) Monte-Carlo Traveling and prizes can be awarded just as with regular Bunkos.

Punched Wins

Many Bunko groups like to keep track of wins and losses by using either a standard round hole-punch, or a designer punch and punching holes in each players score sheet. It is just one more way to customize the look and feel of the game. It is also easy to track "Weighted Scoring" by having a different type of Win/Loss punch at each table. Punched play can use a variety of simple scorecards, from simple index cards to a large paper plate hung around the neck on a string!

Points Play

With Points Play, the points scored in each round are tracked and total points for the night is a prize category at the end of the night. Points play is a little more complex to play and requires a different type of scorecard to play.

Fixed Scorekeeper

The scorekeepers do not change during play. One player is elected (commonly volunteering) to be scorekeeper during play. They keep score for both teams. This is a very common way to play and keep score.

Team Scorekeepers

One person from each team is the scorekeeper, and they keep score for both teams simultaneously. It is very handy to resolve any issues in scoring. This is the most common way to keep score.

All Score

All players have their own scratchpad and keep score of all play except their own. When they have finished their own scoring, their partner tells them the new team scores so they can update their card. This redundant scoring tends to be the most accurate, with little chance of errors happening.

Tables Choice

Each table can decide who is scorekeeper, and whether they use one or two. If anybody at the table would rather have two scorekeepers, and they are willing to be one of them, then the other team has to have their own scorekeeper as well.

Rolling

Rolling options could be grouped under scoring, as they usually influence scoring, but they are directly related to the actual release and capture of the dice.

My Dice

This unusual option doesn't actually change game play. "My Dice" means any player can roll her own "lucky" dice, and a dice cup is passed from player to player to indicate who currently has the roll. This option allows players to develop a collection of personal dice. Personal dice does not work well with any of the Scramble options, and some players believe it slows down the game.

Winner's Dice

With Winner's Dice, one of the players at the table, typically whoever gets to go first, gets to choose which dice to use, and can provide their own. This can be a tricky game, some people playing with under-sized (1/4 inch dice) and oversized (1+ inch) dice just to get an advantage in the speed of play, or to bug their opponents.

Try playing with round six-sided dice and see how many times you roll off the table and lose your turn, if you're not used to them!

Bunko Scramble

Bunko Scramble is a popular option. After anyone rolls a Bunko, all players scramble to grab the three dice. An additional one point is scored for holding each die after a Bunko.

Low Scramble

Low Scramble is very similar to Scramble, except the initial Bunko is only worth 3 points, and each die captured by the rolling team is worth another point. For example, rolling a Bunko and grabbing all three dice afterwards is worth 6 points. Getting two of the dice after rolling Bunko is worth 5 points. If the rolling team only gets one of the dice, they score 4 points, 3 for the Bunko, and 1 more for the die they captured. Note that only the team that rolled the Bunko gets any points.

Split Bunko

Another option similar to Scramble, but the points for the Bunko ONLY go to whoever ends up with the dice. The points for each die in a Bunko are usually either 2 for each die, or 7 for each die. In a game where a Bunko is worth 21 points, holding all three dice after rolling a Bunko is worth 21 points to that team, whether they rolled the Bunko or not. If a team holds two of the three dice, they get 14 points, and the other team gets 7 points.

Stolen Bunko

After rolling a Bunko, all players scramble to pick up the dice. The team that rolled the Bunko only gets the points if they recover two of the three dice. The opponents do not get any points.

Downright-Evil-Aberrant Bunko

After rolling a Bunko, all players scramble to pick up the dice. The team that rolled the Bunko only gets the points if they recover all three of the dice. (If you're playing this version, you may really have gone over to the Darkside! Get Help!!)

Baby Scramble

Baby Scramble is like Scramble, except it is for Baby Bunkos. After rolling three of a kind that is not a Bunko, the players grab for the dice, getting one point for each dice captured, regardless of which team they are on.

Stolen Babies

Similar to Stolen Bunko, all players scramble to pick up the dice after a Baby-Bunko. Each die is worth two points. No points are awarded automatically for rolling the Baby, only for capturing the dice afterwards.

Moving

Moving options result in a non-standard way of moving from table to table or changing partners.

Top Partners

In Top Partners, partners at the Head Table do not change. Whoever your partner was when you won at the Middle Table remains your partner at the Head Table. After winning at the Head Table, you remain with your partner for the next round. This is a very common variant in play.

Descending

Winning teams advance from Low, to Middle to High Tables, as usual. Losing teams descend in reverse order. Losers from the Head Table move back to the Middle Table, and losers from the Middle Table descend to the Low Table. This option results in one more team moving every round, and the Middle Table getting all new players every round.

Free Change

During free change, players are free to move to any chair at the table at the end of the round, as long as they change partners. Players roll to decide who will go first at the beginning of the round. This is the most common way to play.

Pecking Order

Pecking order allows initial seating at the beginning of the game to be determined by the annual ranking. During the year, some prize category (Bunkos, Wins, and/or Points) is tracked for every game, and the seating is done so that every seat at every table is ranked from 1 through 12, and players are seated at the start of play according to their ongoing ranking. This is a very competitive option, but can really be fun. Now the High Table is not just an achievement during the game, but being seated as first roller at the High Table says "That's right, I earned it!"

Arrival

Arrival order to the Bunko party determines seating. The first person to arrive gets the highest seat, the last person the second to lowest. The Hostess starts with the lowest seat. If you are going to play Arrival, you may want to make a rule that 1) No body can arrive more than 15 minutes early, and 2) People who live in the house where the game is being played are seated in order from the bottom seat (number 12) and up.

Losers Walk

In this variation, popular with large groups and fundraisers, the losers at all the tables do the walking, with the winners staying in their place. The losing pair at each table moves to the next lower table, with the losers at the low table moving to the High Table. This negates the value of a having a head table, and should not be played in points play where wins at the head table are worth extra points.

Sidebars

During Bunko play, there can be a number of side games being played. These are often referred to as Sidebars. There is a category of Sidebars that go with drinking games, which are dealt with separately.

With Sidebars, some activity (exchange of a gift, act out an action, steal a prize, etc.) is performed when a certain event happens. There are almost an infinite number of Sidebar combinations, so I will only list some of the most common events and activities.

Gift Exchange

After rolling an Event (for example Kangaroo straight), the roller gets to take a gift from the gift table, or from another player, or exchange their gift if they already have one. A gift can only be stolen from another player a maximum of 3 times, and then it is frozen. Each player can only have one gift. This is popular as a Christmas Ornament exchange.

Take a Buck

Players start with two dollar bills in front of them. The dollars are folded and hidden in two separate hiding spaces, usually under something (coaster, envelope). The players hiding their dollars may choose to place the dollars together in one of the hiding places, or to separate them. When a player rolls the Event (example: rolls a straight) they get to steal the dollars from any other player's cache. Guessing which hiding place has the most money, they will choose one of the two hiding places. After a steal, the two players involved get to re-hide their money.

Dare

Each player is given three items (for example Beads at Mardi-Gras). When an event is rolled, a player can steal another player's beads (1 set). When you run out of your item (beads) you have to perform a dare, if chosen.

Grown-Ups

When an event occurs (for example, baby-Bunko) the player must do some activity that a girl playing grown-up might do. Apply makeup without a mirror; paint their nails with hideous color, etc. The best "Grown-up" at the end of the night wins a prize.

Trivia

Rolling the event gives the roller an opportunity to answer Trivia about the night's theme. Each trivia question answered earns a small prize, or the most correct answers win a prize at the end of the night.

Events:

- ⊡ Roll a pair
- ⊡ Roll any straight
- ⊡ Roll a particular straight (hi 4-5-6, low 1-2-3, etc.)
- ⊡ Roll a kangaroo straight (every other number, e.g. 2-4-6)
- ⊡ Fallen Dice (dice rolls off the table)
- ⊡ Baby-Bunkos
- ⊡ Different colored die rolls the Mark (played with one different colored die)
- ⊡ Different colored die rolls a one or a six (played with one different colored die)
- ⊡ Fourth Die – A fourth die rolled (different type) for a super-Bunko (4 of a kind)
- ⊡ Rolling Snake Eyes (all 1's)
- ⊡ Rolling Big Rig (18 wheeler) (three sixes or 18)
- ⊡ Bad Bunko (players mis-calls a Bunko)

"Qui vino indulget,
quemque alea decoquit,
ille In venerem putret"
{"She who indulges in wine, and is consumed
with dice, wallows away in venal vice."}
Persius

Bunko circles often include social drinking. Many groups have combined Bunko with a variety of drinking rules to make for even more interesting versions of the game.

Bunko and drinking have a long history together. The Bunko Parlor and Speakeasy have long been associated with each other. Who first had the inspiration to mix drinking and Bunko? We'll never know, but it has caught on in a big way. Bunko games in some quarters concentrate more on the drinking rules than the dice rolling rules! These types of games are as common and varied as imaginable. The popularity of Bunko on college campuses may be directly tied to these extreme Variants and Options.

Fortunately, most Bunko parties seem to be neighborhood affairs, and the players can often just walk home after the party. Some circles have designated drivers, or spouses to help those who may have a few too many get home. Another popular choice is to have the players turn in their keys at the beginning of the party, with the hostess hanging onto the keys of people who shouldn't be behind the wheel.

Any way you look at it, please don't drink and drive.

Drinking Vocabulary:

Sip – Sip from your glass, lips must touch liquid
Imbibe (Drink) – Level must lower perceptibly
Chug/Down – Empty your glass, and invert
Two Fingers - A drink from a glass that would lower the contents by two finger-widths

Alternate words for Drink: Imbibe, Sip, Chug, Gulp, Swig, Knock Back, Down, Belt, Swill, Tipple, Quaff, Nip, Guzzle (just to name a few.)

Light-Drinking Options & Variants

The games in this category are divided into light-drinking and heavy-drinking games. The light-drinking games add drinking events to the action, but usually not enough to change the basic nature of the game. They rarely involve "chugging." When a penalty requires drinking, this usually means the level of liquid in the offenders glass is expected to perceptibly lower.

Some groups save the drinking games for the last set of the night. Six rounds of Straights and Confusion are enough so that most everyone will leave feeling little pain.

The number of "~" after an option's name gives an idea to how wobbly you may be walking afterwards.

Bad Babies ~

Rolling a Baby-Bunko, three of a kind of anything but the mark, causes the rollers partner to drink. The roll still generates five points.

Crass (Pinkies) ~

While drinking, the imbiber must keep their pinky clearly extended, and not touching the glass. Failure to do so causes another drink forfeit.

Drunko (Wet Bunko) ~

Person rolling Bunko can make any one other person at the table drink. The person who rolls the Bunko must shout DRUNKO, not Bunko. Shouting Bunko is not considered a False Bunko, but the roller loses his or her opportunity to make someone else drink. The person selected to drink must be sitting at the same table as the roller.

False Bunko ~

Anyone falsely announcing Bunko drinks. The False Bunko may be called because the player forgot what the Mark was, rolled out of turn, or any other reason. Penalty for a false Bunko is commonly more than a single drink, often a chug.

Hot Die ~~

Played with one different colored die, if the odd colored die rolls the Mark, the Roller can make any one other player drink. If playing Wipeout, where one is never the mark, or Christian, where six is never the mark, rolling a one or six respectively, the Roller drinks

Straight, Small ~

⚀⚁⚂ -Usually combined with the Large Straight, and Kangaroo Straight, after rolling a 1, a 2, and a 3, the person on the players left drinks. When all three types of "Straights" are played, the game is often referred to simply as Straights.

Straight, Kangaroo ~

⚁⚃⚅ Usually combined with the Small Straight, and Large Straight - after rolling a 2, a 4, and a 6, the person across from the roller (their team-mate) drinks.

Straight, Large ~

⚃⚄⚅ Usually combined with the Small Straight, and Kangaroo Straight, after rolling a 4, a 5, and a 6, the person on the player's right drinks.

Open Drunko ~

Same as Drunko, or Wet Bunko, except the person selected to drink can be seated at any table.

Pointers ~~

No pointing with the finger is allowed. Players must point with their elbow. If someone observes felonious finger pointing, the pointer must imbibe.

Sloppy ~~

An illegal dice roll (stacked, cocked, falls off rolling mat, falls off table) is grounds for drinking.

Thumbmaster ~~~

Whoever is in possession of the Traveler becomes the Thumbmaster. At any time, the Thumbmaster may surreptitiously place one thumb on the table. All other players at that table must do likewise. The last to do so must imbibe. The Thumbmaster may only do this once per round. If the Thumbmaster is caught doing this twice in a round she is required to double-drink, and loses all Thumbmaster privileges.

Two-Fingers ~~

Any one forced to drink, must drink two fingers worth of their preferred beverage from their (clear) glass. This is not a recommended rule when drinking shots!

Verbiage (Imbibe) ~~

Anyone using the word drink during a round must drink if someone points it out. Acceptable words include Imbibe, Sip, Chug, Gulp, Swig, Knock back, and Down.

Vulgarity ~~

Any vulgarity said aloud forces the pronouncer to imbibe. Hostess or possessor of the Traveler is commonly appointed as the Censor, with final say over what is or isn't a vulgarity.

Wet Traveler ~

Whoever gives up the Traveler, usually by throwing it at the announcer of Bunko or Drunko, must drink after getting rid of the Traveler.

Wet Wipeout ~

Rolling all ones not only wipes out the players score, but also requires them to drink.

Miss Manners ~~~

A shortcut name for a game played with the following options: Imbibe, Pointing, Vulgarity, and Pinkies. Infractions are usually announced formally. *"Miss Thomas, infraction for [Verbiage, Pointing, Vulgarity, Crassness]. Please [imbibe, quaff, sip, etc.]"*

Heavy Drinking Options & Variants

The games in this category can lead to difficulty walking, speaking or staying awake. Play with care!

Bottoms Up ~~~~~

At the end of each round, the losers are required to finish their drinks and refill before the next round (ouch!) Not for the faint of heart. If playing Bottoms Up, I'd recommend using small glasses!

Challenge ~~~~

After a player rolls a Bunko, opponents can challenge the Bunko. They each roll a single die. For each Mark they roll, the Bunko score is reduced by 5 points (maximum of 10-point deduction). For each non-Mark they roll BOTH players on the opposing team chug.

Cumulative ~~~~

After rolling the three dice, a player can re-roll one die if she chugs first, two dice if both partners chug.

Cumulative Extreme ~~~~~

Same as cumulative except the rolling team can choose to have both partners chug, after which the roller re-rolls two dice. The players may then opt to BOTH chug again, and re-roll one of the two dice they just rolled.

Hi-Low Pounding ~~~~

Anyone rolling three ones, chugs, scores no points and continues rolling. Anyone scoring three sixes scores 5 points (unless it is the Mark, then they score the full 21 points) and everyone chugs.

Odds and Evens ~~~~~

Rolling all odd numbers, your team drinks, rolling all even numbers, your opponent drinks. Bunkos and "Baby-Bunkos" are excluded.

Quarters ~~~~

Each time the roller scores one or more points, their partner attempts to bounce a quarter into an upright glass. This requires a hard surface and a reasonable sized drinking glass. A shot glass may also be used, making for a much smaller target. Success allows the partner to select an opponent to drink.

The quarters are usually bounced on their face, although bouncing on the edge may be allowed, particularly by rolling it down the player's nose.

Red, White and Blue ~~~~

⊡⬜⊡ Played with three different colored dice, any time the Mark is rolled on a die, a corresponding player must drink. For example, using Red, White and Blue dice, Red = Player to the left drinks, White = Teammate (player across the table) drinks, Blue = Player to the right drinks. Any three colors can be used; just make sure to specify which seat corresponds to each color.

Redo ~~~~

A player who fails to score on a dice roll can chug their drink to roll all three dice again. This option may only be chosen once per turn.

Wet Confusion ~~~~

(*Warning: This option is complicated!*) Anybody rolling three of a kind that is not the Mark, (a Baby-Bunko,) scores 5 points and selects someone to drink (the Drinker). The Drinker then gets to roll a single die. If they roll the existing Mark, they chug. If they roll the same number as the Roller rolled three of, the Roller chugs. For any other number, that number becomes the new mark, and the Drinker must take that many drinks from their glass. The Roller gets to continue their turn.

Wicked Doubles ~~~~~

After rolling a pair of the Mark and any other number, the third number indicates who drinks.

⚀ - The person to the roller's left drinks

⚁ - The person opposite the roller drinks

⚂ - The person to the roller's right drinks

⚃ - The person to the roller's left drinks twice

⚄ – The person opposite the roller drinks twice

⚅ – The person to the roller's right drinks twice.

If the odd die is the current Mark, the player rolling joins the other person in the drink.

Forfeits

Many games are played with forfeits. Forfeits are used when a player does not want to perform their drinking duties, or when specific events call for them to come into play. They are most commonly included at social events, for example, when Drunko is played at a larger party, or in a public location such as a bar.

Forfeits can be as tame or wild as you want. Your imagination is the limit. Examples of some typical party forfeits are:

Musical

Musical forfeits may be done with extra provisos such as without smiling or while standing on one leg.

Sing or whistle:
- The National Anthem
- Happy Birthday
- Humpty-Dumpty
- Baa-baa Black Sheep
- Mary had a Little Lamb
- Do the little Teapot song & dance
- (We all live in a) Yellow Submarine
- Eat three crackers - without having a drink - then whistle a song, which others have to recognize

Dancing
- Do the Twist
- Do the Macarena
- Get someone to join you in the Chicken Dance
- Belly Dance
- Limbo under a bar

Speaking

- Recite a poem of your choice
- Recite a Children's Rhyme
- Recite a limerick
- Say the days of the week backwards
- Say the months of the year backwards
- Recite the Alphabet backwards

Acting

- Do an impersonation of John Cleese being Basil Fawlty
- Do an impersonation of Mel Gibson being William Wallace
- Perform from Shakespeare
- Act like a chimpanzee
- Act like a chicken/hen/rooster
- Act like a snake
- Act like a puppy

Quiz or list

Answer some preset questions such as:

- Name the Spice Girls
- Name the seven dwarfs from Snow White
- Name the planets of the Solar System
- Name ten things you would find in the kitchen
- Name ten things you would find in the bathroom
- Name ten parts of the human body with only 3 letters
- Name ten things you can stroke in public.

Dares

- ☐ Shake hands with everyone
- ☐ Kiss a bald man on the head
- ☐ Kiss someone wearing glasses
- ☐ Wear a **false** moustache and wig for the rest of the game
- ☐ Wear a **silly** hat for the rest of the game

Clothing

- ☐ Remove an item of red clothing
- ☐ Swap socks with the person on your left
- ☐ Wear your clothing inside out
- ☐ Wear your shirt backwards.

Drunko!™

Unlike Bunko, Drunko is not usually played for prizes. It is a social drinking game with the primary goal of getting your friends more inebriated than you. Winning will keep your drinking level down, while losing can have a detrimental effect on your sobriety.

As easy as Bunko is to play, Drunko is even easier. Good thing, with that much quaffing going on!

Team Drunko! ™

The Official Rules of Team Drunko™ - A Bunko Dice Drinking Game

Materials:
- At least 8 players, 12 players are recommended.
- 1 table per 4 people
- 3 dice per table
- 1 scratch-pad per table
- 1 score card per person
- 1 Bell at the Head Table (for starting and stopping rounds)
- 1 soft, tossable item (Fuzzy Die, stuffed animal, etc.)
- 1 Drinking glass per person (minimum)
- Sufficient quantity of the alcoholic beverage of choice

Rule 1: Score Points by Rolling Three Dice

The object of the game of Drunko is to win rounds of play by out scoring your opponents, while encouraging them to imbibe alcoholic refreshment. Players score by rolling three dice and matching the current number or Mark, which has been established for that round. Players take turns rolling the dice. A player continues rolling as long as they score one or more points per throw.

Point scoring is as follows:

- ⊡ 1 die showing the Mark = 1 point.
- ⊡ 2 dice (or doubles) showing the Mark = 2 points
- ⊡ 3 dice showing the current Mark = Drunko = 21 points
- ⊡ 3 of a kind dice (triplet), of any other number = 5 points

Rule 2: Drinking Rolls

Of the three dice rolled, one is of a different color. This die is referred to as the "Odd" die. If that die shows the mark after a roll, the following drinking penalties occur:

- Odd die only show Mark = Roller chooses opponent to drink.
- Odd die and one other show Mark = Both opponents drink.
- All dice show Mark = Drunko! = The roller can choose one player, at their table or any lower table, to chug.

In addition, if two dice show the mark and neither is the odd die, the roller's partner is required to drink.

Rolling three of a kind of any number other than the mark = Roller chooses one player from their table to drink.

Rule 3: Legal Rolls

In order for a roll to count, the dice must be lifted off the table, shaken and rolled on the table. Dice scores count only if the dice land cleanly. If the dice land stacked or cocked, the roller is required to imbibe of their drink, and all three dice are re-rolled. If any of the dice fall on the floor, the roller is required to imbibe their drink, and all three dice are re-rolled. If the dice fall off the table twice during one players turn, the roller and their partner chug and that ends their turn.

Rule 4: Ranking Tables and Teams

One table is designated the Head Table. The Head Table controls the pace of play. The other tables are assigned an arbitrary order from lowest to highest.

When rolling a Drunko, players can be made to drink at the same table or any lower one. For example, let's look at 3 tables in play, a High table (controlling play), a Middle Table, and a Low Table. If a Drunko is rolled at the Low table, anyone from that table can be made to Drink. If a Drunko if rolled at the Middle table, the roller can select anyone from their table or the Low Table to drink. Finally, if a Drunko is rolled at the High table, the roller can choose to have anybody that is playing drink. In all cases, this can include their partner.

Rule 5: Initial Setup

Initially, players choose their table and seat at random. Dice are rolled at each table to determine who rolls first. The Host or Hostess starts with possession of the Traveler token. Each player should be provided a drinking vessel, clear or translucent if preferred. The drink of preference for the evening should ideally be present at each table.

Rule 6: Keeping Score

The rolling player's partner is the scorekeeper and is tasked with keeping score on a score pad. There is no specific manner in which this scoring must be kept.

Scorekeepers may use scratch paper, mechanical counters, or any other device they deem appropriate. At the end of each player's roll, the scorekeeper adds the player's score to the running total for their team, and announces the new team score. Failure to announce the score is an infraction, and if the other team rolls before the scorekeeper announces the new score, he may be deemed "Tardy" and is required to drink. If the opposing team does NOT announce the "Tardy" infraction, no drinking is required.

Rule 7: Establishing the Mark

During play, the game is played in Sets, which consist of 6 rounds. The Mark (point to be rolled) for each round is established at the beginning of that round, and is announced by the initial scorekeeper at the Head Table. The Mark starts at 1 and advances by one up to 6, matching the number of the round within the set. E.g. Round one, the Mark is 1. Round two, the Mark is 2, and so on up to Round six, where the Mark is 6. Announcing the Mark is a courtesy and no penalty is incurred if the scorekeeper fails to announce the Mark.

Rule 8: Thumbmaster

Drunko is played with a "Thumbmaster" token, commonly an ornamental hat, fuzzy die or other item, called the "Traveler". When a player rolls a Drunko (3 of the Mark), the current keeper of the Traveler throws it towards whoever rolled the Drunko. Any rolling of a Drunko, including rolling at a lower table after the Head Table has announced the end of the game, such as during a roll-off, is valid for exchange of the Traveler. The possessor of the Traveler becomes the Thumbmaster, until the next Drunko is rolled.

Thumbmaster Rights: At any time, the Thumbmaster may surreptitiously place one thumb on the table. All other players at his table must do likewise. The last to do so must imbibe. The Thumbmaster may only do this once per round. Caught doing this twice during the same round forces the Thumbmaster to double-drink, and lose all Thumbmaster privileges. The Thumbmaster is not required to "thumb the table" during any round.

Rule 9: Playing the Round

At the start of each round, players roll 1 die to see who goes first. The round begins with a signal from the scorekeeper at the Head Table, usually by ringing the bell, and the players at each table begin the rolling. A round is completed when one of the teams at the Head Table scores at least 21 points. The current scorekeeper announces the end of the round again by ringing the bell, and the turns end at all tables. No score is allowed if the dice have not touched the table when the end of the round has been called, with the exception that all players are entitled to roll at least once.

Rule 10: Wins and Losses

When either team at the Head Table scores 21 they have won the round. At the lower tables, whichever team has the most points when the rolling is ended, wins the round. If there is a tie at one of the lower tables, play continues as normal until one of the teams score and break the tie. After all rolling has been completed, each player from the losing team is required to imbibe. The amount imbibed is in relation to the table they are sitting at. The amounts are:

- **Low Table**: Losers quaff 2 fingers of their drink
- **Middle Table**: Losers quaff 1 finger of their drink
- **High Table**: Losers imbibe of their drink

Rule 11: Advancing Tables

When all scores have been updated players change places and teams. Players from the winning team at the lower tables advance one table rank towards the Head Table. Losers at all the lower tables remain at that table, the last person to roll at the table changing their seat. The losers from the Head Table move to the lowest table. At the lower tables, each player should have a new partner. At the High table, the partners do NOT change seats, and the team moving up from the middle table will stay together, to confront the reigning champions.

Rule 12: End of the Game

The players should decide ahead of time when the game will end. This may be at a selected number of Sets (3 or 4 is common), at a predetermined time, when a certain number of players have dropped out (or been dropped), or when the beverage of choice has run out. When the game is over, players who can still walk help their friends who cannot!

Common Drunko Options

Drunko is often played with the following options:

Verbiage: Using the word "Drink" and its derivatives is not allowed and the offender must drink.

Pointing: Pointing with a finger is prohibited and the pointer must drink.

Fingers: Whenever a person is required to drink, a clearly perceptible amount must be consumed. For example, if "one finger" is specified, the level of the beverage within the glass must go down approximately the width of one finger (about ½ an inch.)

Common Drunko Lingo.

While playing Drunko the following terms are commonly used for events in the game.

Barney: Odd die showing the mark = roller selects one person to imbibe

Twins: Odd die and one other showing the mark = opposing team drinks

Annie (Orphan): Two dice, neither one the Odd die, showing the mark = Partner drinks

Abuse: Spilling the beverage is grounds for drinking.

Laggard: Last person to follow the Thumbmaster's lead.

Individual Drunko™

Team Drunko is very similar to Bunko. Individual Drunko™ or just "Drunko" plays a good bit different.

Drunko is played at one large table, and it is every woman (or man) for herself. The game is fast paced, with each person's roll an attempt to get someone else to drink. The game is played until the predetermined end is reached.

Rolling a Wipeout (three ones) is commonly an opportunity for a nature-break, and refill.

Drunko ™

The Official Rules of Drunko™ - A Bunko Dice Drinking Game

Materials:
- Less than 8 players
- 1 table large enough for all
- 3 dice – each a different color
- 1 soft, tossable item (Fuzzy Die, stuffed animal, etc.)
- 1 Drinking glass per person (minimum)
- 1 Additional Drunko glass (suitable for playing quarters)
- 1 quarter
- Sufficient quantity of the alcoholic beverage of choice

Rule 1: The Mark

The Mark (point to be rolled) for each round is established at the beginning of that round. The Mark always starts at 6. Rolling the Mark on a particular die creates a drinking event, and after the drinking is completed, the roller gets to roll again.

Rolling three of a kind of any number other than the Mark or ones, reverses the direction of play, and the number rolled becomes the new Mark. The player rolling continues to roll with the new Mark.

Ones cannot be the Mark, and are handled separately (see Wipeout).

After failing to roll a mark, the roller passes the dice in the appropriate direction, and must imbibe from their own drink.

Rule 2: Drinking Rolls

Three different colored dice are rolled. These dice are named. The colors can be any, but the role of each colored die is determined before the game starts.

- **Chooser** - The Mark rolled on this die entitles the roller to make any one person at the table drink
- **Loser** - The Mark rolled on this die causes the person who last rolled a Wipeout (three ones) to drink.
- **Boozer** - The Mark rolled on this die requires the person who is seated the same number of seats away from the roller, in the direction of play, to drink.

Rule 3: Legal Rolls

In order for a roll to count, the dice must be lifted off the table, shaken and rolled on the table. Dice rolls count only if the dice land cleanly. If the dice land stacked or cocked, the roller is required to imbibe of their drink, and all three dice are re-rolled. If any of the dice fall on the floor, the roller is required to imbibe of their drink, and all three dice are re-rolled. If the dice fall off the table twice during one player's turn, the roller chugs and their turn ends.

Rule 4: Drinking Quantities

If the Mark is rolled on only one die, the person who has to drink is required to 'imbibe', i.e. the level of their drink must lower perceptibly.

If the Mark is rolled on two dice, the people who have to drink must quaff "a finger", i.e. the level of their drink must lower by one finger's worth. A finger's worth is considered the width of a finger, or about ½ an inch.

If the Mark is rolled on all three dice, the roller announces "Drunko" and the Loser and Boozer must quaff "two-fingers" while the Chooser must chug their drink.

Rule 5: Wipeout

Rolling three ones constitutes a Wipeout and ends the roller's turn. The person rolling the wipeout takes possession of the "Loser" token, commonly a Bar-Towel or soft fuzzy tossable item. They are then required to finish their drink, and they become the "Loser".

Rolling a Wipeout is commonly chosen as a break in play, for a nature call, or for refilling drinks etc.

Rule 6: Drunko

Rolling three of the Mark constitutes a Drunko. The person rolling the Drunko takes possession of the Drunko Glass and becomes the Drunko Master. Whenever the Mark is rolled in the future, the Drunko Master is entitled to attempt to bounce a quarter into the Drunko glass (as in the "Quarters" option) and when successful, can select one person at the table to imbibe.

If the current roller rolls the Mark on two dice, the Drunko Master will get two opportunities to play Quarters.

If the current roller rolls the Mark on three dice, or Drunko, the current Drunko Master does NOT get to play quarters, but immediately passes the Drunko Glass to the new Drunko Master.

If the Drunko Master is ALSO the current roller, they do NOT get to enforce their Drunko Master rights during their rolling.

Rule 8: Playing the Round

At the start of each round, players roll 3 dice to see who goes first. The highest roll gets to go first. The lowest roll becomes the "Loser". Ties for high and low roll have a roll-off, until a clear First-roller and Loser are determined. There is NO Drunko Master at the beginning of play. The direction of play begins clockwise.

Rule 9: Entering and Leaving the Game

Any player can leave the table in Good Standing at any time, so long as:

1) They are not currently required to drink
2) They are not currently the "Loser" or Drunko Master

Any player can enter the game at any time as long as:

1) They have not played before or they left the table in Good Standing
2) The must imbibe two fingers to take a seat

Any player who is NOT in good standing, and desires to enter the game must chug or pay a forfeit (see Options) to re-enter the game.

The Loser may only leave the game in good-standing after convincing someone else at the table to take over the role of "Loser". The Drunko Master may only leave the Game in good standing after appointing another player to be the Drunko Master.

Rule 10: End of the Game

The players should decide ahead of time when the game will end. This may be at a selected number of Sets (3 or 4 is common), at a predetermined time, when a certain number of players have dropped out (or been dropped), or when the beverage of choice has run out. When the game is over, players who can still walk help their friends who cannot!

Options and Variants:

Drunko can be played with most of the options and variants listed previously in this chapter.

"I read Shakespeare and the Bible, and I can shoot dice. That's what I call a liberal education."
Tallulah Bankhead

Starting a new Bunko Circle is easy enough in theory. Find at least seven other people, 11 preferred, who would like to get together once a month to socialize, eat, drink, and play Bunko!

If you don't have 11 friends chomping at the bit to play, you might try sending a flyer out to friends and neighbors. Something like:

LET'S PLAY BUNKO!

We are starting a BUNKO NIGHT for the neighborhood.
BUNKO is a dice game that is easy to play. No experience needed.
Expect lots of FUN and LAUGHS.
It's a great opportunity to get to know your neighbors!

When: 2nd Tuesday of the month, starting May 10th, 7:00-9:30PM
Cost: $5 per person towards prizes for the evening
Where: Ellen's house (123 Lemon Rd)

Call to join or with questions:
Jules at 555-1221 or Karen at 555-2112

RSVP by Monday, May 1st

Other groups have had a lot of success using the internet, especially www.meetup.com. Using **Meetup** will cost a few dollars. You can get started for $19.00 for one month, and then cancel the group once you have your players. If you want to continue to have an internet group site, you can use something free services like Yahoo Groups (groups.yahoo.com) or www.BuncoCentral.com to organize your group.

You may end up with more than 12 people. That's Ok. You can play with 16 or even 20. If you have an odd number of people, you use one or more 'Ghost' players to even up the numbers.

At your first game night, you will have several tasks ahead of you.

1) Decide on the rules of the game. For the first game, I'd suggest using a standard version of the game, such as Progressive Bunko. Print out copies of the rules for each table. You can find sample material you are welcome to print out and use at the end of this book.

2) Explain the rules of the game. I'd suggest you use the cheat sheets I've provided. Then play a Set, with open questions while playing. There is a good chance a few of your players may have played before. If so, separate them and try to have at least one experienced player at each table.

3) Once you've played a Set, take a break and try to find out who would like to be a full time member of the new Bunko circle, and who is interested in being a substitute. Have your guests fill in a roster. (More about that later).

4) Find a volunteer from among your new full-time players, and schedule the next game. You'll want to discuss when the best night of the week to play the game is.

5) Play the rest of your Sets, liberally interspersed with beverages and snacks, and distribute the prizes at the end of the night.

6) Turn over your Bunko Box of materials (dice and bell, scorecards and roster) to the hostess of the next party.

You're well on your way to starting a successful Bunko Circle! Congratulations!

One Thing You MUST Do

Want to know one of the best aids to keeping your Bunko gatherings a long-term success? It's not necessarily what you may think. It is not the night you choose to meet or the number of people who attend. While important, it is not the type of food or snacks you serve, or even the themes you develop.

What is it?

It is as simple as a group roster! Your roster may be the single most important element in the ongoing success of your group, and is a key to building your group and keeping it organized and together. Groups who have been Bunko'ing together for many years share this handy tool to stay on track.

Roster Essentials

First, pull together a list of all players, both regular and substitute. Include contact info like phone numbers and addresses. This is critical so that the host/hostess can make contact with all players prior to game night, reminding them of that all-important gathering.

Windsor Place BUNKO Group

Date	Hostess	Address	Phone	Appetizer	Dessert	Side
1/5	Anna S.	2324 London	555.1234	Donna	Gina	Jensen
2/13	Bev. L	4533 Heathrow	555.3544	Erin	Hannah	Kelli
3/13	Cheri T.	3312 Kennsington	555.9823	Francis	Ivana	Tricia
4/11	Donna N.	8812 Buckingham	555.3424	Gina	Jensen	Anna
5/10	Erin A.	2939 Heathrow	555.2934	Hannah	Kelli	Bev
6/15	Francis F	8231 Pickadilly	555.8822	Ivana	Tricia	Cheri
7/13	Gina M.	7712 Heathrow	555.2174	Jensen	Anna	Donna
8/12	Hannah M.	2326 London	555.5885	Kelli	Bev	Erin
9/10	Ivana B	3434 Buckingham	555.7703	Tricia	Cheri	Francis
10/15	Jensen P.	8931 Kennsington	555.1109	Anna	Donna	Gina
11/13	Kelli K.	4522 Danforth	555.3294	Bev	Erin	Hannah
12/12	Tricia P.	8931 Kennsington	555.1109	Cheri	Francis	Ivana

SUBS	Lori B.	Mary K.	Mna Q
	555.9892	555.8988	555.6543

Second, list the future meeting dates (and times, if they change periodically). If your group has predetermined who is hosting games throughout the year, include this on the roster. It is highly valuable because it helps everyone to plan better. Babysitters, shift changes at work, or any other scheduling adjustments work best when they can be planned well ahead. If a monthly player sees a conflict due to vacation, work, etc., a substitute player can be sought in advance so they can plan to take their place. This increases the chances of having a full house on Bunko night.

Third, keep it current. If someone moves or dates change, update the list and redistribute a copy to everyone. Check in periodically with your substitutes to ensure their information is current too. If you can, try to inspect the list 2-3 times annually for current content.

Finally, enlist someone in your group to "own" the roster responsibility, and rotate that responsibility annually or periodically. It is a simple task that, while not overly time consuming, is important never the less.

Many groups have learned to let technology work for them. They maintain their rosters and calendars on the internet, making it easy to access, share and update. If you have any web-divas in your group, you may want to look into going this route.

See Appendix D for a sample Roster Sheet, and other useful game materials.

Establishing Rules

Ok, if maintaining an accurate and up-to-date roster is the number one key to a successful Bunko group, clearly spelled out rules run a close second. You can avoid some hurt feelings and bickering just by having as much as possible spelled out ahead of time. Here is a way to get started.

Write Down Your Rules

Bunko is an easy game to play, and a much harder game to define on paper. Nevertheless, the effort spent here will pay off in the end. Your group should discuss the rules they want to play by, and document them. The following are the basics:

EZ-Bunko OR Progressive Bunko?

Will your group set a simple Mark, usually sixes or ones, or let the Mark follow the round number? If you're playing EZ-Bunko, how many rounds will you play per set? How many sets will you play each evening?

Suggested Rules:
1. The game is Progressive Bunko, as defined by The Bunko Book, with the Mark matching the round number.
2. Game play is three sets of six rounds each.

Points Play

Will your group track the points in every round, accumulating their score all night long? Many groups like to play for points, awarding "Most Points" the top prize for the night.

Suggested Rules:
1. We do not play for points

Traveling

Does your group want to play with the Traveling rule, using a cash cup, a tossable toy, or some other special item to track the last player to roll a Bunko? It usually adds a good bit of screaming, getting up and down from the tables, and a whole lot of fun.

Suggested Rules:
1. We play with Traveling. Last player to roll a Bunko gets "Fuzzy" tossed to them.
2. Whoever has "Fuzzy" at the end of the night, wins the "Traveling" prize.
3. The Hostess, at her discretion, may replace "Fuzzy" with any thematic Traveling item, for the evening.

Wipeout

Will your group play wipeout, where rolling three ones (or sometimes three sixes) wipes out your current score? Groups that play wipeout almost invariably award a prize to the last person holding the wipeout item, whether it is a crying towel, a fuzzy die, or some small stuffed animal.

Suggested Rules:
1. We do not play with wipeout.
2. The Hostess may choose to include wipeout play at her discretion, but any Wipeout prizes may not come from the standard prize pool.

Unspecified Rules

Suggested Rules:
1. In the case of any rule questions, the Bunko Book will be our reference for play.
2. The rules of Progressive Bunko from The Bunko Book are superseded by any previously documented house rule.

There are lots more options and variants you can choose to use. My best suggestion is to decide which rules you are going to play by, and declare that for all non-specified rules, you will follow a set of "Official Rules." You may choose to use the rules printed here, the rules from the World Bunko Association, the rules in your "It's Bunko Time" box, you can even use the rules listed online at www.BuncoBook.com.

You may decide you would like to have a review of the rules, every 6 months to a year, to see if there are any changes desired. Most groups are much less formal, throughout the year they fine-tune the way they play, and they frequently try different options and variants just to see what they are like. Other groups have played with the same exact rules for 20 years or more!

In Appendix B of this book are several variations in game rules. Your Bunko Circle is welcome to use any of these rule sets as the basis of your game play. You can make as many copies as you like for your game use.

Any way you decide to go, document the rules, get everyone to agree to them, and follow them. Too many groups have broken up over the interpretation of game rules, and over prize distribution. Write it down. Write it down. Write it down.

Did I mention, **Write it down?**

Playing for Prizes

When you form your group, one of the big decisions you will need to make is how much to charge to play and what kind of prizes you will play for. For the first event, I recommend a simple $5.00 fee, and providing prizes for:

- Most Wins
- Most Bunkos
- Last Bunko (traveler)
- Most Losses
- Consolation Prize

Collect the money at the beginning of the night, and make sure everyone understands how the prizes are distributed. For the first night, I would recommend that nobody be allowed to win more than one prize.

The prizes awarded can be cash or prizes purchased by the hostess. For the first night, cash awards are often best, since you're probably unsure how many players you'll have.

During one of your breaks, the group should decide how they want to play in the future. This is probably the biggest single decision. Will your group play for cash or for prizes? How much will you pay each evening? This simple decision often effects the other decisions. Cash groups are usually less likely to play *Wipeout*, are more likely to play *Scramble*, and typically have fewer prize categories. You may want to lay some ground rules about how much extra a hostess can ask anyone to bring. It is not uncommon for a hostess to say bring an extra dollar or two, but on occasion some hostesses have as much as doubled the nightly fee or more.

There are many variations out there for prize play so I thought I'd at least document some of the most common ways of setting this up.

Paying in

If you are going to play for prizes, the best way I've found is to have the regular players contribute each month for the **next** month's prizes. The hostess for the next month will take the money and purchase the prizes for the next party. The first time you play, you will contribute double: once for that first night, and once for the next meeting.

Most groups do not ask the substitutes to pay when playing for prizes. It is up to the regular player to pay for the game, even if they cannot make it.

Many Bunko Circles play for cash prizes, in which case it is not necessary to pre-pay the upcoming game. You contribute the night you play - and bring cash! Most cash groups for some reason usually have fewer prizes, higher payouts, and they take the play a little more seriously. Substitutes pay their own way; you play you pay.

The most common amounts of contribution are $5.00 and $10.00, in that order.

Bunko FACT: Most people play for cash.

71% of Bunko Circles play for Cash Prizes.
80% of the groups pay in **$5.00 each**.

Categories of Prizes

Prizes at the end of the night can be based on any one of a number of possibilities. Wins, Losses, best costume for a theme night, most potty breaks, you name it, people play for it.

If you choose to set up award categories, here are some of the most common categories groups have used:

- Most Bunkos
- Most Wins - person with most **W** (Wins)
- Most Losses - person with most **L** (Losses)
- Equal Losses and Wins
- Most Wipeouts
- First Bunko
- Traveling - Last person holding Bunko Traveling fuzzy die
- Traveling Wipeout - last person holding Wipeout crying towel
- Consolation prize - selected randomly from everyone who didn't win a prize

Clearly, there are a huge number of ways you can combine the prize value with the categories of prizes available. Most circles seem to like to distribute a lot of prizes, at least 5 to 7, whereas most cash prize circles lean towards having a couple of high pay-outs, making the game a lot more competitive in nature (and often resulting in chants of "C'mon baby, momma needs a new pair of shoes").

I have found the overall favorite prize distribution to be:

- Most Bunkos = $20
- Most Wins = $15
- Most Losses = $10
- Traveling (Last Bunko) = $10
- Consolation (Random draw) = $5

The following awards categories are some of my other favorites - based on a five-dollar entry, and twelve players. To read the chart, select any column. For that column, the prize category on the left pays the amount indicated.

Based on $5 Kitty fee	Winners & Losers	Everyone Wins	Travelers Delight	High Payout	Straight Bunko	Bunkos Rule
Most Bunkos	20	15	20	30	20	15
Most Wins	15	10	15	20	15	10
Most Losses	10	5	10	10	10	5
Traveling	5	5	10			10
Wipeout	5	5	5			5
2nd Most Wins		5			5	
Losses=Wins		5			5	
First Bunko		5				10
Consolation	5	5			5	5

Bring a Gift, Get a Gift

Bring a Gift, Get a Gift is a fun variation, which makes sure nobody goes home empty handed. On top of the regular $5 donation, each person brings a small wrapped gift of less than $5 or $10 value.

When you roll Bunko, you have an option. Either select a gift from the gift table (where all the gifts are originally stored) or "steal" a gift from someone who has already picked.

If your gift is stolen, you pick a new one from the gift table. You can't steal someone else's just because yours has been stolen. Unless, of course, you roll your own Bunko!

You can only have one Gift. After you've already selected a gift, if you roll another Bunko, you have the option of exchanging gifts, either with another person or with the table.

Appendix B has printable Prize Rules you are welcome to use.

You Don't Have 12 Players?

For Bunko, the ideal is to have 12 players, seated at 3 tables. Eight players and two tables work well, as does sixteen players and four tables. More than that can get unwieldy, but I know many people that play that way.

But what if you have 11 players? Or 14?

This is where the "Ghost" comes in.

The Ghost is a pretend player, usually represented by a stuffed animal or something similar. The Ghost will move around like a regular player, but the Ghost's partner rolls for the Ghost. Scoring for the team is just like a normal team with one exception - the partner gets credit for any Bunkos that are rolled for the Ghost.

You can even play with 2 ghosts, just make sure they are not partnered together!

If you have one player more than you need, playing with three Ghosts can become a problem. Instead, it is better to have one player sit out each round. Typically, this would be one of the players that moving from the High Table to the Low Table. Just roll two dice, with the loser sitting out the round. This way nobody is likely to sit out more than one round out of every four or more.

I have seen many interesting Ghosts over the years, including pillows, large stuffed animals, picture frames, and even photos of absent players. Be creative!

Fixed Ghosts

As an alternative way of handling the Ghost, some people play with the Ghost(s) being permanently seated at the bottom table.

With only one Ghost, if the team playing against the Ghost wins, they move up to the next table, and the Ghosts partner moves as is partnered with one of the two people who will sit at the table next. If the person partnered with the Ghost wins, she moves up to the next table, and the two remaining players have a roll-off with one die to see who moves up with her.

With two Ghosts, win or lose, both players move up to the next table.

> "Death and the dice
> level all distinctions."
> *Samuel Foote*

A Bunko group or Circle should typically consist of 12 players. It is important to have all twelve players available for a night of Bunko. Most groups have 12 starters and several alternates. It is the responsibility of the regular starter who cannot attend a game night to find their replacement. If a replacement cannot be found play may continue (using Ghost rules, see Chapter 7 and the Frequently Asked Questions section.)

The 12 regular starters take turns hosting the party. The hostess is given a Bunko box, containing game paraphernalia, which may be as simple as 9 dice, or as complex as the team desires. The hostess should set up 3 tables for four, ideally with some type of soft covering, felt or a heavy tablecloth, to minimize the noise of the dice rolling and the bouncing of the dice.

With 12 players playing once a month, each player will host the party once a year, and will usually be required to supply a snack or entrée once every 3 months - except the month they are the hostess.

Eating, Drinking and Bunko

Snacks and drinks are a mainstay of Bunko. The hostess may be asked to provide the snacks, but more commonly, the Hostess provides non-alcoholic beverages, while 2 to 3 players are tasked with bringing snacks.

When providing snacks, a common setup is to place one bowl containing a sweet snack and one bowl with a salty snack at each table. M&M's and Chex-Mix seem to be a standard requirement.

Drinking is a common part of Bunko, and it should be advertised that for any alcoholic drinks it is BYOB. Again, some circles take pride in drinks such as specialty Margaritas or Daiquiris, and it seems that wine is the preferred drink of most circles. If you are drinking, it is likely that the end of each round will require "potty breaks". If you have smokers in the group, you may also want to have a "smoke break" at the end of every three rounds (including between sets).

For many groups meals are the heart of the Bunko Night. In this case, the Hostess provides the main course, and three other players provide 1) a side dish, 2) an appetizer, and 3) a dessert.

Under normal routines (once a month play), each player will host the event once a year, including providing the main course, and will have to provide snacks/sides/dessert once every three months.

If the food is going to be more than snacks, the breaks should be preplanned. For example, appetizers may be served before the game starts, the main course after set one (six rounds) and dessert after set two.

However you plan to handle the food, discuss it and make it a standard way of doing it. Some groups have gotten into one-upmanship duels as to who can outdo her rivals, while other times the parties have been held with little more than water served to a group of 11 who arrived hungry expecting dinner. Set your expectations.

Setting up for play

Set up the three tables with enough room for everyone to move around. Bunko is a social game as much as a game of luck, and most groups have lots of getting up and moving around (see Traveling - under game options) both during the game and between rounds. If you have the space, placing small folding trays at the corners of the table you're playing at can leave more room for play, especially if you're playing Scramble (see options) and want to keep the drinks off the floor.

If you like to have everything nice and orderly, here is a way to deal with the chaos of initial seating and getting ready to play.

Place three dice, a Bunko Table-Tally score sheet, and pencils on each of three tables. Place a table placard (Low, Middle, High), on each table. Place the four sequentially numbered seating placards, in front of each chair. A bell is placed on the High Table. If you're playing with Traveling, a large fuzzy die (or a small stuffed animal) is placed on the Low Table.

Prepare 12 Bunko scorecards by writing on the back of them. Four are labeled HIGH table, with the numbers 1, 2, 3 and 4. Four are labeled MIDDLE table, 1 through 4, and four are labeled LOW table.

Players select a scorecard at random when they arrive and sit in the indicated place. Partners for the first round are the players sitting across from each other.

The events of the night should be announced at this point (when breaks will occur, etc.) and play starts with the ringing of the bell at the Head Table.

A minimalist version of the same setup might go as follows: Set up three tables. Place a bell at one table, which becomes the high table. Place the traveler fuzzy-die at another table, which becomes the low table. The remaining table is the middle table. Leave a notepad (or two) on each table with a pencil and three dice. Have the players grab a personal scorecard when they arrive and they can sit wherever they want. This results in a first-come, first-served type of seating arrangement.

It doesn't get much simpler than that.

Hostess Etiquette

The following monthly checklist is suggested for the Hostess who wants to make sure she will have a successful Bunko Party.

Two Weeks Out

___ If you are having a theme party, email the players with the Theme.

___ If your theme needs supporting goodies, order them early. Websites such as OrientalTrading.com, BunkoGameShop.com, and DiceGamers.com have lots to help on your big day.

Three to Four Days Out

___ Remind the players (phone or email) of the upcoming party, and their responsibilities, if they are supposed to bring a dish etc. Remind them of the theme as well, if any.

___ Remind your husband/housemate/significant-other of your game, and make sure they will be absent (unless it is Couples-Bunko night)

___ Arrange for an off-site baby-sitter if needed. A movie outing with dinner might be appropriate. You may be able to unload your kid(s) at one of the other member's houses.

Day Before

___ Follow up with anyone who indicated they might have a problem making the game. Ensure they have a substitute if possible.

___ Shop for any prizes you need.

___ Shop for any groceries / drinks you will need.

___ Remind the others in your household they will need to be gone tomorrow.

Day of the Event

___ Decorate for the theme if needed.

___ Prepare your dishes early.

___ Kick everyone out of the house that's not playing!

___ Setup your tables and game items.

___ (Optional) Get an early start by testing the drinks.

Your Bunko Box

It is important to have all your basic materials together. I'd suggest that you create a Bunko Box. In it, you keep your dice, bell, scorecards, scratch paper, pencils, punches (if you use them), your Traveler(s), a copy of your Roster, and a copy of your rules. At the end of the night, the Bunko Box is passed on to the next hostess.

It is the hostess's responsibility to make sure that the Bunko Box is complete, and that there are enough scorecards and scratch-pads for play.

Changing Game Play

Many groups permit the hostess to make small rule changes to the game, particularly with groups that encourage theme nights. You may want to adapt the game to the particular theme you are playing.

It can be great fun, but I would suggest you don't stray too far from the group's core rules. Changing the Traveler to match the theme, or adding appropriate 'penalties' are great ways to go.

If you are going to change the rules significantly, especially if you're going to ask for more money for the "kitty", make sure to let the other players know ahead of time.

Bunko Fact: When it comes to rolling three of a kind that is not a Bunko, players show a lot of imagination. Sure, baby-Bunko, Monte Carlo, or Babies, might be what we call it here in The Bunko Book, but many dare to be different! The favorite **50** alternative names we received were:

aces, almost, anti-Bunko, auto, blooper, bonus, boob, boobie, boos, bunny, butthead, chunko, crap, cupcake, drunko, duck, extra, fake, farkel, free-roll, freebie, frog, gizmo, goose, gunko, half, hat-trick, jackass, kisses, lucky, natural, non-bunko, oknub, odd Bunko, on the town, pseudo, quarters, same, skunko, small Bunko, smiley, spoons, suito, trixie, troll, unnatural, wanna-be, woopie, wipe-out, yahtzee

---

"The devil is in the dice"
Old English Proverb

The sad fact is that any competitive game will bring out the worst in some people. There are players whose behavior and mere presence can make the game miserable for everyone. Worse yet, there are those who have to win at all costs.

Would people really cheat at a game like Bunko? You bet they will. People cheat at Monopoly when nothing is on the line. Most of the time there is an opportunity to go home a little better off then how you arrived at Bunko parties.

The stories I have heard range from horrible, through disheartening, to just plain ridiculous. The only real solution against cheating is to be aware, recognize the signs, limit the opportunity, and bring it to an immediate halt.

Cheating will occur in two basic formats, scoring, and rolling. Let's deal with scoring first.

You rolled how many Bunko's?

If you follow the recommended scoring method laid out here, and use scoring cards similar to those presented, you will have done 98% of what's possible to stop cheating. However, I know that there are many different methods of keeping score, and I'd like to point out some of the problems inherent therein.

Self-scoring

This is the number one problem that enables cheating. Certainly, we want to trust everyone, and since every player carries around her own scorecard, it is easiest if she just tracks her own score. Easiest is not always best.

When teammates manage each other's scorecards, the cheating disappears! Some tables have the opposing players at each table mark the score on the other players cards.

> **Bunko Fact:**
>
> 86% of Players use notepads to keep score
> 10% use printed scorecards
> 2% use punch cards
> 2% use some other means to keep score

Warning – warning – warning!

Because of the mobile nature of the game, and the difficulty in tracking game play, as well as the constant changing of partners and which table they played at, if people are going to score their own cards, you need to track which round and which table each win occurred at, as well as each Bunko. If someone claims that she rolled four Bunkos and she only rolled three, it is hard to call them out. On the other hand, if they claim they rolled a Bunko at the Middle Table, during Set 1, Round 2, then the other players at the table for that game can provide validation for claimed scores.

Tracking the round can be done in many fashions, whether it is by using a labeled score sheet, colored pencils at each table, or different punches for winning and losing at each table. Here is what I have found to be the best way to do each.

Labeled Score Sheets

If you are using labeled score sheets, you should have a place to mark each win, and which round and set it occurred in. In the examples on the right, the scorecard is configured for four sets of 6 rounds. The rounds are scored vertically, next to the dice image which matches that round number (and the Mark for that round as well.)

Bunkos should be marked in the round they were rolled. In the first example, the Bunkos are tracked at the top of the scoresheet, whenever they are rolled. In the second example, the die icon is colored in or overwritten whenever a Bunko is rolled. Now we know in which round, and which set each Bunko was rolled. It is obviously a lot easier to verify the second scorecard over the first.

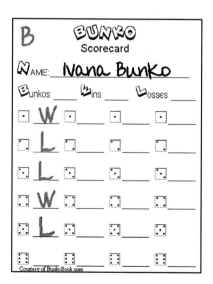

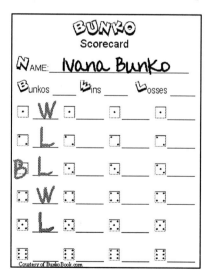

BUNKO
Scorecard

NAME: Nana Bunko

Round	Point Tally	Pts	W/L	B
⚀	~~JHT~~ III (B) II	31	W	1
⚁				
⚂				
⚃				
⚄				
⚅				

Courtesy of BunkoBook.com

If you are playing with point scoring, you might use a scoresheet similar to the one on the left. You can use the space next to the round number to track your scoring as you roll. Rolling a **B**, is 21 points, and can be totaled at the end if you are not at the High Table.

Circle the B if you rolled it, and leave it un-circled if your partner gets credit for it. Now how can anyone make a mistake on this scorecard, and not stand a good chance of being caught at the end?

Different Colors – Different Tables

You don't need fancy scoresheets to make scoring easy and reduce the likelihood of cheating. In this example, using a truly minimalist approach to scoring, at the end of each round a player marks a W or an L on their score sheet. What makes it easy to track the scoring is that losing scores are always marked in red, and each of the tables has a different color pencil/marker to mark wins. In this example Blue is for the High Table, Green is for the Low Table, and Lavender is for the Middle Table.

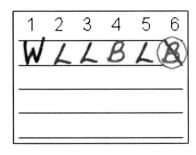

To track Bunkos just mark a B in the column under the round you are currently playing, in the table color.

At the end of the round, the winning team will share the colored pen to mark their sheets before leaving the table, and the losing team will share the Red pen to keep their score.

I highly recommend this easy way of tracking wins and losses. It is relatively painless, and almost always eliminates any "mistakes" in scoring.

Flavored Punch

Punching a card is a very popular way to keep score. One way is to take a common index card, start in one corner and work your way around the edge, six punches to a side.

Each table can use a different "flavor" of punch, or you can optionally just use one kind for wins and another of losses.

In this example, a yellow highlighter is used to show where to start the scoring. Then a punch is used at the table for wins and losses. A plain circle punch indicates a loss, and any fancy punch indicates a win. Here we use a star to show a win at the High Table, and a Triangle to indicate a win at the Low and Middle Tables. Bunkos are tracked by writing a B next to the round you are currently playing, far enough in so that it will not be punched at the end of the round.

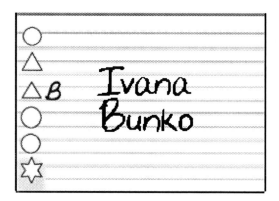

The secret to punching is to have punches for wins and losses. Some groups only get a punch when they win, and then it's hard to know when the win occurred. By using wins and losses and following a pattern, you'll be sure to leave a trail of wins and losses that can be backtracked at the end of the night, should any "fishy" scoring occur.

Scoring Your Teammate

This is the simplest thing you can do to minimize cheating in terms of wins and losses. If you just exchange scorecards before each round with your new partner, and at the end of the round, mark the Wins and Losses on each other cards, people usually don't "accidentally" mark a **W** where an **L** belongs.

The problem of mis-marked Bunkos stills exists of course. The best solution is the same as listed for self-scoring, make sure that Bunkos are marked somehow indicating the Set and Round in which they occurred, so they can be independently verified if necessary.

Another interesting alternative included tying a different colored marker to the Traveler. The only way you could mark a Bunko on your scoresheet was to have the Traveler in your hands. It may not eliminate all issues, but it seems to help.

Issues with Rolling.

You would be amazed. Once for demonstration purposes I rolled the current point eleven times in a row, including two Bunkos, just to show it can be done. And I'm not some kind of magician or card sharp. Controlling the rolls is surprisingly easy and even easier to get away with if no one is looking for it.

There are two ways to cheat while rolling. One is to use crooked dice. There are numerous places you can get dice that are weighted, shaved, or mis-marked in order to roll the numbers you want. Call it a gift from the game of craps.

In Bunko, this is typically not a huge problem because of the nature of the game. Passing dice around the table means if the dice are going to roll nice for you, they'll also roll nice for the people you are playing against. Now of course it is possible that the local cheater is an expert at palming the dice in and out of the game during their roll, but the truth is, if they are that good, they're going to get away with it. Sorry.

Also, the fact that the number you are trying to roll is constantly changing, means you would need many different loaded dice to win consistently.

The only time that crooked dice would likely be a problem is if you have a constant point (for example, your Mark is always six) and players can roll their own dice. In this event, it would be pretty easy to have one loaded die that rolled sixes a little more often. Using colored, opaque dice, a drill and a little molten metal, this would take about 5 minutes to do, good enough to pass a casual inspection.

The message here is this: if you are going to play a fixed Mark game, do not let people roll their own dice.

The real problem comes in the roll of the dice.

The Dreaded Whip Shot and Other Trick Rolls

If you study craps and "dice-setting", you will find that a lot of effort has gone into getting an edge in dice rolls, in a situation where a LOT of effort has gone into making sure you can't cheat.

In the case of Bunko, there is no wall to roll against; no requirement to roll a certain distance, and quite often no one is really watching that carefully. This spells opportunity for anyone with even a passing knowledge of dice manipulation.

I do not intend for this book to be a manual on cheating at dice rolls, but it seems relevant to demonstrate the most common methods of cheating while rolling, and some simple solutions to prevent it.

The most common methods of cheating when rolling dice are well documented by John Scarne, in his book *Scarne on Dice*. The three methods I have found most commonly used during my investigation are the Blanket Roll, The Whip Shot, and The Stacked Roll.

The Blanket Roll

The blanket roll is the easiest and probably most common way to improve your odds while rolling Bunko dice.

Hold the dice so that they are one straight bar, three dice, side by side. Then make sure that the number you want to roll is NOT on the side of the dice that are facing each other. When you roll the dice, roll them off your fingers so that they roll straight, end-over-end. Done properly, your chances of rolling the number you want is now 1 in 4 instead of 1 in 6. Like the improved odds?

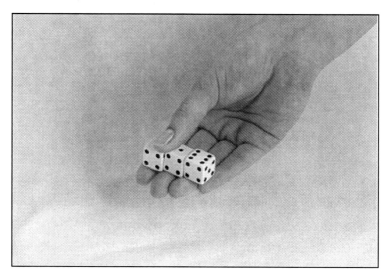

The Blanket Roll – Going for fours

When someone rolls the dice from their hand in this fashion, you should insist that the dice be shaken before they are rolled and the dice need to roll randomly, not end over end. Insisting that the dice are dropped from at least 6 inches above the table helps as well.

Another view of the Blanket Roll

The Whip Shot

The Whip shot is only a little harder, and can improve your odds even more. Rolling the Whip Shot is how I demonstrated how easy it is to cheat to a room full of Bunko'ers. The way that one particular group looked at one of their members lead me to believe it was not the first time they had seen that roll.

With the Whip Shot, the dice are stacked so that the number you want to roll is on the top of each of the dice. Then the dice are whipped out of the hand, with a side-hand toss, so that the dice tend to slide across the surface, rotating, but not rolling over. The top dice will have a greater tendency to tumble, but it is easy to consistently make the bottom die keep the chosen face up.

In practice, you would actually probably only stack the bottom die, and you would allow the top dice to tumble naturally. In this way, the dice seem to fall naturally, but careful observation will show the die nearest the roller doesn't tumble, but slides across the surface, and is the most likely to roll the Mark. The cheater will usually pick this die up with the side of their hand, and keep the point up, so they do not have to do any kind of setting of the dice after they have picked them up. With practice, you can roll the dice quickly and smoothly, and roll the Mark repeatedly.

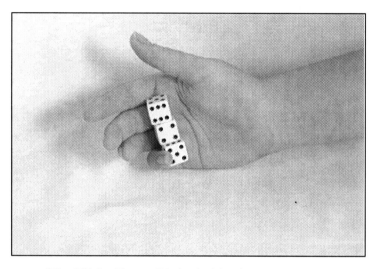

The Whip Shot – Pinky holds the one we want

Again, if you see the dice sliding and not tumbling, insist that the dice are shaken, and rolled so that they ALL tumble. You can also watch for how the player picks up the dice. If the last die they pick up each turn is showing the mark, it can be an indicator of something crooked going on.

The Stacked Roll

The stacked roll is the least consistent, but one of the hardest to detect. The dice are stacked, just as with the Whip Shot, but they are tossed down at the surface so the upper-dice pin the bottom die to the surface. It will often stick with that face up, while the other dice tumble away.

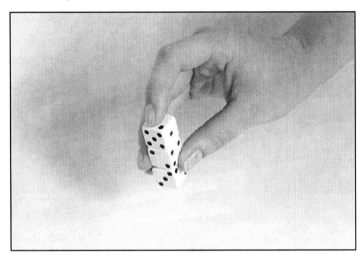

The Stacked Roll – Downward Throw

The hold is a little different from the Whip. Usually the dice roller will use one finger on top to add an additional impetus to the downward thrust, to make the dice hit the surface while they are still all connected, improving the odds that the bottom die will stick.

The throw appears a little unnatural when observed. The dice will also usually have an extra loud clatter when they first hit. If you see someone stacking the dice for "good luck" and throwing them straight down, insist on the dice being shaken, and that all the dice tumble. (I know, I am sounding repetitive.)

The Simple Solution

With all this rolling stuff, how can you make sure the game is played fairly? One of the easiest ways is to use a dice cup. Dice cups have been used for almost as long as dice games have been played. It is much harder to control the dice when using a dice cup. Yes, it can be done, but the amount of effort usually required to do so is just not worth it.

As long as you require the dice cup to be held with the open side up, shaken and then the dice poured out or the cup inverted, you will eliminate virtually all opportunity for cheating on the roll of the die.

Using a cup can slow the game down a little, but it can be almost as fast, and it also allows the users to each roll their own dice for fun (just pass the cup, not the dice). Of course, if you use a cup and decide to let the players roll their own dice, watch out for the loaded dice. A way to avoid loaded dice is to allow a player to use the same dice that the last person used. Alternatively, allow the person who starts the rolling to select the dice, but make everyone use the same ones for that round.

Try it. Using the dice cup and your favorite dice makes for a cleaner and often wilder game.

> "I have a notion that gamblers are
> as happy as most people, being al-
> ways excited; women, wine, fame,
> the table, even ambition, sate now
> & then, but every turn of the card
> & cast of the dice keeps the gam-
> bler alive - besides one can game
> ten times longer than one can do
> any thing else."
> *Lord Byron*

A very popular Bunko side activity is to base your monthly Bunko night on a theme. These can follow holidays, seasons, school, or any other reason you can think of celebrating.

Hostess Choice

Choosing to hold a theme or not is usually the hostess's choice, unless it is a special occasion, such as a fundraiser, or an annual event. It is also the hostess's responsibility to let everyone know everything they need to for a successful party.

Once a group has determined the prize payout, it shouldn't be changed substantially by the hostess. However, the hostess can ask players to pay-into a special prize pool. If she does take this route, she should give fair warning in the invitation, and do not make it more than one or two dollars.

If the Bunko night is a theme party, the hostess may also want to have some small prizes that are theme oriented, but again they shouldn't cost more than a few bucks.

Recipe Cards

If you are having an unusual recipe, or if you're experimenting with some special drink for the evening, you may want to go ahead and prepare some recipe cards with the drink/meal recipe. If the experiment is a success, you WILL be asked for the recipe, and it is always better to be prepared.

Assorted Theme Nights

There have been many discussions on Internet Bulletin Boards and Forums about how different groups play. The following theme descriptions come from these accounts of what some groups are doing today, as well as some original ones.

Bunko Fact: *Theme nights are common*

More than **84%** of Bunko Groups surveyed play with an occasional theme night.

Valentine's Day

Costumes: Any trip to Victoria's Secret should give you plenty of ideas!

Atmosphere: Fill a basket with red cellophane shreds and red foil-wrapped heart-shaped milk chocolates. Instead of glitter or confetti around the base, throw around those little heart-shaped candies with sayings like, "Be Mine".

Try using small stuffed animals for centerpieces. At this time of the year, you can often find bears, rabbits, lions, tigers, pandas and more, all holding "I Love You" hearts. Afterwards, you could donate them to a local children's hospital or shelter.

Food: Serve food dyed in colors of pink or red. Chocolates (kisses are especially popular) are great. Provide a valentine decorated cake, with hearts or cupid. Serve pink punch. For table snacks, have conversation hearts, Valentine color M-n-M's, red pistachios, and/or an assortment of valentine candies.

Game Ideas: If you have ever thought about hosting a "Couples" Bunko party, this is a great opportunity. Just remember, you're going to need double of everything. There are many different ways to play large group Bunko. A popular couple alternative would be to play as you would normally, and then at the end of the night the couples add their points together. Prizes can include dinner gift certificates, movie tickets, and his and her gifts.

You will often find that men often do not understand the simplicity of the game and will try to find a strategy behind the play. Expect rushed rolling, questions about holding onto the dice, and other strange stuff.

Mardi Gras

Costumes: Encourage everyone to dress up in fancy attire and wear eye masks. You could even provide materials for each person to create their own masks. Beads are a must, and if you look hard you can find some nice dice beads.

Decorations: Hurricane cups, Mardi-Gras chocolate coins, beads galore, fancy fringed table skirts, colorful metallic colored balloons and jeweled crowns can all add to a Mardi-Gras feel for your party.

Food: Serve some New Orleans style snacks or a real Cajun meal. You could refer to your iced shrimp as crawdads. Serve a special "king" cake complete with a luck baby inside. Of course, genuine French Quarter Hurricane punch is necessary. For table snacks, have (multi-colored) M-n-Ms or Skittles, hot spicy peanuts, and beaded candy.

Game Ideas: The beads and a crown make ideal replacements for fuzzy dice. Instead of having a Traveling Bunko die, use a Bunko crown, or a special oversized set of beads. Bead tossing contests could be another possibility. You might try a "stealing" game, where rolling a straight, or a baby-Bunko, entitles you to steal a set of beads from someone else. When you are out of beads, you may have to perform a dare to get another bead necklace.

St. Patrick's Day

Costumes: Anything green of course.

Atmosphere: Outside your door entrance, place a Blarney Stone for people to kiss as they walk in. When they do, they should make a wish. Any large, CLEAN, rock from the backyard should do just fine. Attach a sign that says, "BLARNEY STONE...kiss here and make your wish!" Shamrocks, and black pots full of gold (chocolate) coins, can give an Irish feel to the room. "Luck o' the Irish" and "Kiss me I'm Irish" buttons are fun. You might want to attach a lucky shamrock to your own collar so that luck-of-the-Irish will be with you!

Food: Serve Corn Beef and Cabbage, or perhaps an assortment of corn beef sandwiches. A baked potato bar, with a variety of stuffed potato fillings is also a lot of fun, and easy. For beverages, nothing beats Irish (green) beer or a green dyed punch, except maybe a dash of Irish whiskey, or Bailey's Irish Cream. For table snacks, pistachios, gold chocolate coins and assorted green candies of course. Irish coffee makes a perfect ending to any St. Patty's Day Bunko Party.

Game Ideas: Have everyone add the prefix "Mc" or "O" to their last name and use it all night long, with penalties for failing to use the Irish version of anyone's name. Have everyone bring quarters, and during the game, anyone who rolls three ones tosses a quarter into a leprechaun's pot o'gold, and has to wear a Leprechaun's hat. Whoever is wearing the hat at the end of the night gets the pot of gold! Exchange a Shillelagh for the Traveling die, and make the last person to roll a Bunko carry it around and talk with an Irish Brogue.

Cinco de Mayo

Costumes: Colorful, playful skirts and peasant shirts are great. Sombreros of course have their place. Ponchos and Flamenco outfits can be fun as well.

Atmosphere: Decorate in red and green. Piñatas make great inexpensive decorations, and can be given out as prizes at the end of the night. Mexican sombreros make great centerpieces. Can you still get Mexican Jumping Beans? Crank up the south-of-the-border tunes, including La Bamba, Tequila, and La Cucaracha.

Food: Prepare and serve Mexican dishes or snacks. Make-it-yourself tacos are ideal and fun. For drinks consider Margaritas (virgin or the real kind), Mexican Beer, even Tequila shooters for a rowdier crowd. For dessert, a flan is always the choice. For table snacks, after the obvious chips and salsa, and guacamole, have Red-hot Tamale candies, pistachios, and multi-colored M&M's. Remember, red and green! Kahlua and coffee makes a nice after dinner drink.

Game Ideas: Winners have to do a Mexican Hat Dance to claim their prize. For the Traveling die, use a giant Sombrero the roller has to wear. Encourage everyone to wear ponchos and use thick accents. Guess who is Mexican – 20 questions about famous Mexican personalities with small prizes. Encourage a "sensual señorita" costume party with a prize to the best costume.

Fourth of July

Costumes: Red, White and Blue. Flag shirts, or anything else you can think of that's generally patriotic.

Atmosphere: Streamers in Red, White and Blue, and lots of flags are the obvious. For a patriotic theme, a Capitol building, fireworks, and Uncle Sam all make for nice decorations. Balloons are a must. Try a patriotic face painting session at the start of the night.

Food: Fire up that Barbecue! BBQ ribs or hamburgers, potato salad, and corn-on-the-cob make for a true blue American meal. Apple pie with homemade vanilla ice cream can finish things nicely. Any American brew will do, although Sam Adams seems particularly apropos. For table snacks, try peanuts, popcorn, and Cracker Jacks!

Game Ideas: For an interesting variation, play a trivia game where each player is secretly assigned an original colony at the beginning of the evening. Each time a person rolls a straight a progressively easier clue is announced as to which State they are. Players try to figure out who all the players are. First person to figure out the missing State wins a prize. First person to figure out which state everyone is (or whoever gets closest at the end of the evening) wins a prize. Get some antique looking parchment, write up the Bunko Constitution, and have each State representative add her own John Hancock to it.

Oktoberfest

Costumes: Aprons combined with long skirts and plain white blouses are simple additions that really give an authentic look. Lederhosen, dirndl, jackets, vests, long socks, and strappy sandals can all provide a German feel to your costume. For the adventurous, traditional German outfits can be rented at any costume rental.

Atmosphere: Cobalt blue and Snow white are the official colors of Bavaria, home of the original Oktoberfest. Consider holding the party outdoors, just as they do in Munich! Decorate with dried flowers and wheat. Geraniums are popular in Bavaria. Get posters of Germany from a local travel agent and adorn the walls with them. German flags and crests from the 16 German states make great decorations. A bouquet hung from the ceiling, with streamers radiating out to the walls is an inexpensive but authentic look. Of course, it is not Oktoberfest without the music. You might even pass around Kazoos so the players can play along.

Food: There is nothing more authentic than German sausage, with sauerkraut, and German beer. For a little more elegant fare, you might try wiener schnitzel or roast pork. Did I mention German Beer? Potato pancakes make a great appetizer, with applesauce, and warm cider makes for a nice treat. Black Forest Cake and German Chocolate Cake are terrific desserts.

Game Ideas: An inexpensive Tyrolean hat can usually be found in a dollar store and makes a great Traveler.

Seasonal Ideas for Themes

This should give you some ideas for your own theme night. Below I've included some more seasonal ideas.

January = New Years, Inauguration, Australia Day (for our friends "Down Under" – put something on the Bar-B), Super-Bowl

February = Valentines (Co-ed with hubbies), Presidents, Groundhog Day, Chinese New Year

March = Easter, International Women's Day, First Day of Spring

April = April Fools, Daylight Savings, Jelly Bean Day, Arbor day, Spring Break

May = May Day, Cinco de Mayo, Mother's Day, Armed Forces Day, Memorial Day

June = Flag Day, Father's Day, National Gingerbread Day, School's Out, Start of Summer

July = Fourth of July, Canada Day, Lazy Summer Days

August = Friendship Day, National Aviation Day, Back to School

September = Labor Day, Grandparents Day, Flower Week, Citizenship Day, First Day of Fall

October = Columbus Day, Canadian Thanksgiving, Sweetest Day, Halloween

November = Veteran's Day, Remembrance Day (Canada), Thanksgiving, Election Day

December = Christmas, Hanukkah, Boxing Day, Poinsettia Day, Winter starts, School Break, New Years Eve

Random Ideas for Themes

We've discussed the idea of theme parties that are tied to holidays, or seasonal events, and given you some examples to get your creative juices flowing.

There are only so many holidays, however. An even richer source of themes is our day-do-day culture. There are so many places you can go for ideas to have a unique theme party, I almost don't know where to start.

Here are a few general ideas that you can work with, and some more detailed themes to give you some ideas.

Slumber party: Eye masks, Pajamas, warm socks, robe
Bath time: Fancy soaps, lotions, bath oils, beads, and gels
Garden time: potted plants, flowers, garden tools, garden gloves, fancy pots
Tea Party: Fancy teas or coffees, teapots, cups, mugs, cookies, breads, scones, sugar cubes
Summertime: Suntan lotions, aloe, sunglasses, beach towels
Spa day: gift certificates for a manicure, facial, pedicure, haircut
Drinker's month: any top shelf liquor...Absolut, Grey Goose, Cognac, Brandy, Kahlua, nice wines.

Bridesmaid Bunco

Good theme for anytime of the year but June is a popular wedding month

Costumes: Have everyone wear an old bridesmaid dress or a mother of the bride dress (the uglier the better - give a prize for the gaudiest) have the winner of the gaudiest gown throw a bouquet so someone else can win a prize too.

Atmosphere: You could make a wishing well from a cardboard box for the gifts for the game twist. Decorate with a birdcage with two doves in it, fancy wine glasses, table place setting cards, bubbles at each table. Have a disposable camera at each table and allow players to take candid shots of the "guests". Small little bubble bottles at each seat. Have a little gift for each person at her table. (Maybe a wedding bookmark or make Hershey Kiss roses.) Have a bottle of champagne at each table. If you are creative, you could make an arch of some kind.

As guests arrive, have them take their name table cards to find out where they are seated. At the tables, you can have a ring bearer's pillow, a basket of flowers, pastel almond candies and/or Hershey's Hugs and Kisses.

Food: You could serve a typical wedding meal, like a chicken breast, twice-baked potato, vegetable, roll, salad and sherbet for dessert. A wedding cake would be appropriate.

Game Ideas: Scorecards could be any wedding design or a lovers design or honeymoon setting. For a Traveler a blow-up male groom is pretty wild. A bouquet of flowers or small teddy bears in bride-and-groom costumes are easy to find. Have each player bring a wrapped dollar store gift for the wishing well. Each player that rolls a Baby-Bunko gets to select a prize from the wishing well; when all prizes are gone from the well they can steal from each other. Give a bouquet of flowers to the winner of the ugliest bridesmaid dress and allow her to throw it to the others (since she is soooo ugly she may never get married). Have everyone ring his or her champagne glasses when someone yells Bunko.

Cinderella Ball

Costumes: Have players wear formal gowns. Old brides-maid dresses work well or go to your local thrift store and find a used "Ball Gown". Remember, the gaudier the better.

Decorations: Fine china (or Chinette), crystal and of course cloth napkins and napkin rings yield the look we are going for. You could have pumpkins, crowns, tiaras, glass slippers etc. If you are going for a classy feel, white and lace are all-purpose decorations. Music of a classical nature is most fitting. If you are looking for the more romantic, lean toward the Valentine's Day flavors, with pink, red and white colors, and hearts incorporated into your designs.

Food: Serve hot appetizers, pasta noodles in a cream sauce, green salad, bread and petit fours for dessert and wine or champagne to drink. Chocolate mousse, fancy fruit cups serve well. You may want to go for the 7-course meal, interrupting your play every three rounds instead of every six, for your next course. If you go that direction, you will definitely want to assign as many courses to your fellow Bunko'ers as you can get them to do.

Game Ideas: A Tiara makes the ideal traveler, as does a glass-slipper (a little harder to find.) For a change in the game, buy some heart (love) or lips (kisses) stickers and whenever someone rolls two of a kind (a couple), they get to place a sticker on their shirt or score card. The person with the most stickers at the end of the evening wins a prize. You might also want a prize for the person who got the least love or kisses.

> "Gambling with cards or dice or stocks is all one thing. It's getting money without giving an equivalent for it."
> *Henry Ward Beecher*

Looking for an interesting and fun way to raise money for projects and organizations? You might try what numerous other groups have, a Bunko FUNd-raiser. Your Bunko event may take a little effort to setup, but the payoff can be well worth it. Here is some information you may find useful if you plan to organize your own FUNd-Raiser.

Bunko Fact:

The biggest Bunko fundraiser, *Bunco for Breast Cancer*, has raised more than **$500,000** since 2002. If you would like to participate, check out their web site:

http://www.bcrfcure.org/

Tips for Organizing Your Bunko Event

Planning for a large crowd can be difficult and putting together a fundraising event of any sizable caliber takes effort, BUT it is certainly a new way to convince folks to donate to your special cause. Here are some pointers I have collected from several groups who have braved the challenges of putting together a Bunko fundraising event.

Getting it Organized

Begin well in advance; 6 months to a year is ideal. Determine a fundraising goal, set up a committee of volunteers, and set a date. Pick a location that will accommodate your crowd size; halls work best, and if they are free it's even better! Keep in mind that when choosing a date, the earlier in the year is better and during the middle part of a week (say Tuesday - Thursday) seems to produce the best attendance.

Several committees seem to provide the best results. A couple of local groups recently sponsored events, and they split up their effort along these basic lines:

Sponsor Committee: Responsible for getting prizes and sponsors.
Game Committee: Gathers all game materials – except for tables and chairs, and runs the actual game night event.
Setup Committee: Finds the locations, gets tables and chairs, and finds volunteers to setup and teardown the day of the event.
Food and Drink Committee: Organizes and Sells refreshments (beverages and snacks).
Promotion Committee: Gets the word out! They may want to coordinate the sale of tickets to the event.

The Devil's in the Details

You will need **lots** of game supplies (dice, score sheets, pencils, etc.), tables/chairs and more. A published set of "official rules" used for the night and a printed program listing the schedule, prizes, and donors, should be made available. In your program, it is helpful to include the game and break times so your event flows smoothly and interruptions are minimized.

For game supplies, you can use the sample rule sheets at the back of this book. They may be freely copied and distributed.

Raising the Funds

Possible sources include; entrance fee, live or silent auction, raffle prizes, selling of food & beverages, and sponsorships. A lot of time and planning in this area will net you solid results; giving you a grand assortment of appealing items that will surely attract the buyers and the bidders. Do not shortcut this stuff; it will improve your bottom line in the end.

Some groups have charged a reasonable fee for game play ($5-10) and then issued a raffle ticket for each Win and Bunko. The same tickets could be purchased for $.50 each or 3 for $1. Prizes from sponsors were then distributed based on a raffle draw.

Promoting your Event

Spread the word via press releases, posters, flyers, radio/media, and word of mouth. Recruit ticket sellers for your event and enlist their assistance in selling a specific number of tickets (i.e. 10-20 tickets per ticket seller). Often this is the most effective way to increase attendance. Encourage veteran Bunko attendees to bring a friend who has never played! Convince people to buy out a table (or even a pod!) and let them fill in the group.

Rules for Large Groups

There are many ways to play Bunko as part of a fundraising event. To cover all of them would take an entire book on its own. I am going to cover the most basic form of fundraiser play while keeping one thing in mind - Keep It Simple.

Vocabulary:
Seating: place for 4 players to play. This may be one table, or it may be an arbitrary division at a table.

Pod: The tables within which a number of players, typical 12 or 16 will move. Each pod can be identified by their table numbers.

Round: One turn of play where player teams try to outscore their opponents.

Mark: The number the players try to roll each round.

Set: Six rounds.

Break: The time between each round when players change seats.

Intermission: The time between sets, when players take an extended break between play.

Bunko: Rolling three of the Mark. Players will be awarded a Bunko Token to track the number of Bunkos they roll.

Unlimited Prize Play Bunko

With Prize Play, the layout of the tables is not critical. The players are divided up into arbitrary groups at random and move within their groups. A single Head Table is selected, usually out of a "By Invitation" pod. Players seated at this pod are typically Guests of Honor, or win their seats through auction, purchase or other invitation.

The players at the Head Table control the play as in standard Bunko, and the round ends when a team at that seating scores 21 or more points.

Players can be seated either at the typical tables of four, or at long tables which are commonly able to seat eight players.

If you have many card tables, and are able to seat all your groups at tables of four, the easiest way to move the players around is to group the tables into pods of three, and label each table with its pod number and a seating ranking. For example, tables 1A, 1B 1C, 2A, 2B, 2C and so on. Within each pod, A is the Head Table, and C is the Low Table. At each table, the players sitting across from each other are partners. At the end of each round, players will move within their pod just as in regular game play. At the end of the set, you will have one winner for each pod (12 players).

If you are using long tables, break the tables up into seatings of four at each table (two seatings to a table is typical). The players will sit in a grouping of four, two on each side facing each other. Partners sit diagonally across from each other. It is easiest if you make two long tables a complete Bunko pod, and limit the players' movement to those 2 tables. You can then label the seatings as 1A, 1B, 1C, and 1D at your first two tables, and 2A, 2B, 2C and 2D at your next two tables, etc. Seating 1A is the High Seating and seating 1D is the Low Seating. Winners advance from seating 1D to 1A. Losers at seating 1A move to seating 1D at the end of the round.

The same holds true for all pods. At the end of the set, you will have one winner for each pod (4 table seatings, 16 players).

Volunteers are responsible for passing out Bunko tokens each time someone rolls a Bunko. They are also responsible for punching the winner's cards at the end of each round.

Other than this, play is very similar to Progressive Bunko.

Unlimited Bunko

The official rules of Unlimited Bunko, as used with very large groups.

Materials

- ⊡ As many players as desired, divisible by 4
- ⊡ 1 table seating per 4 players
- ⊡ 3 dice per table seating
- ⊡ 2 or more scratchpads per table seating
- ⊡ 2 or more pencils per table seating
- ⊡ 1 score card per person
- ⊡ 1 volunteer for each group
- ⊡ 1 winner's punch per volunteer
- ⊡ Numerous Bunko Tokens per volunteer (10 per set is plenty)

Rule 1: Score Points by Rolling Three Dice

The object of the game of Unlimited Bunko is to win rounds of play by out scoring your opponents. Rolling three dice and matching the current number or Mark, which is established for that round, is how a player scores. Players take turns rolling the dice. A player continues rolling as long as they score one or more points per throw. Point scoring is as follows (example is for Round 2, making the Mark 2):

⊡⊡⊡ 1 die showing the Mark = 1 point.

⊡⊡⊡ 2 dice (or doubles) showing the Mark = 2 points

⊡⊡⊡ 3 dice showing the current Mark = 21 points

⊡⊡⊡ 3 of a kind of any other number = 5

Rolling three of the Mark is a Bunko, scores 21 points, and the player must announce the Bunko aloud.

Rolling three of any other number is a Baby Bunko, scores 5 points, and the player gets to continue rolling.

Rule 2: Legal Rolls

In order for a roll to count, the dice must be lifted off the table, shaken and rolled on the table. Dice scores count only if the dice land cleanly. If the dice land stacked or cocked all three dice are re-rolled. If any of the dice fall on the floor, all three dice are re-rolled. If the dice fall off the table twice during one player's turn, that ends their turn.

Rule 3: Pod Seatings

Tables of Four: Tables are divided up into "Pods" of three tables, for a total of 12 players. Each pod makes up one standalone Bunko group. Teammates sit opposite each other. Within the Pod, One table seating is designated the High Seating. The other table seatings are assigned an arbitrary order from lowest to highest. There may be any number of Pods in play during the event.

Tables of Eight: Tables are divided up into "Pods" of two tables, for a total of 16 players. Each pod makes up one standalone Bunko group. Each table has marked "Seatings" of four players where teams will play against each other. Teammates sit diagonally across from each other. Within the Pod, One table Seating is designated the High Seating. The other table seatings are assigned an arbitrary order from lowest to highest. There may be any number of Pods in play during the event.

Rule 4: Initial Setup

Players select their seating at random. Dice are rolled at each seating to determine who rolls first.

Rule 5: Keeping Score

The rolling player's partner is the scorekeeper and is tasked with keeping score on scratch paper. There is no specific manner in which this scoring should be kept. Scorekeepers may use scratch paper, mechanical counters, or any other device they may deem appropriate. At the end of each player's roll, the scorekeeper adds the player's score to the running total for their team, and announces the new team score. Any player who rolls a Bunko should announce the roll, and receive a Bunko Token from their grouping volunteer.

Rule 6: Establishing the Mark

During play, the game is played in Sets, which consist of six rounds. The Mark (point to be rolled) for each round is established at the beginning of that round, and is announced by the game hostess. The Mark starts at 1 and advances by one up to 6, matching the number of the round within the set. E.g. Round one, the Mark is 1. Round two, the Mark is 2, and so on up to Round six, where the Mark is 6.

Rule 7: Starting the Round

At the start of each round, players rolls one die to see who goes first. In the case of a tie, those players have a roll-off until a starter is determined. The round begins with a signal from the Game Hostess, usually by ringing a bell, or sounding a horn, and the players at each table begin the rolling.

Rule 8: Ending the Round

A round is completed when players at the single Head Table score 21 points. The Game Hostess announces the end of the round again by ringing the bell or blowing the horn, and the turns end at all tables. No score is allowed if the dice have not touched the table when the end of the round has been called, with the exception that all players are entitled to roll at least once.

Rule 9: Tracking Wins and Losses

Once the end of the round has been announced, the team at each seating that has the most points when the rolling is ended, wins the round. If there is a tie at one of the seatings, play continues as normal until one of the teams score and break the tie. After all rolling has been completed, each player from the winning team should receive a punch on their scorecard from the group's volunteer official. Players from the losing teams will not receive a punch.

Rule 10: Advancing Tables

When all scores have been updated, players change places and teams. Players from the winning team at the lower seatings advance one seating rank towards the Head Seating, within their pod. Losers at all the lower Seatings remain at that table, the last person to roll at the table changing their seat. The losers from the Head Seating move to the lowest seating. No one should play with the same partner twice in a row.

Rule 11: Game Breaks

Breaks are taken between rounds, to allow players time to get their scores tallied, and to move between seatings. After the third round of each set, an extended break is taken to allow for bathroom breaks and drink refills. Between sets an extended break is also held, with time enough for activities such as food and drink breaks, silent auction perusal, and any other personal needs.

Rule 12: End of the Game

The Tournament ends after 3 sets of play. At that time, final calculations are performed and prizes are distributed.

Common Prize Distributions are:
- Top Three Bunko Counts
- Top Three Most Wins
- First Bunko
- Last Bunko

Common Fundraiser Options and Variants

Fixed Mark

To keep game play as easy as possible, a single Mark is selected and rolled for the entire evening. For Fixed Mark, six is the most common Mark. When using a Fixed Mark, it is easy to change the number of rounds per set as well.

Traveling

Fundraisers usually do NOT use a traveler due to the confusion and noise level.

Wipeout

Wipeout is a popular option among Fundraisers, especially when combined with the fixed Mark. With wipeout, rolling all ones results in a wipeout, and the player's team score reverts to zero and their turn ends. When playing with wipeout, tracking wipeouts in the same way as Bunko's and awarding a Most Wipeouts prize is common.

10-Point Bunko

Some groups prefer to award fewer points to a Bunko in large group play. 10 points is a common point award for a Bunko.

No Babies

With this option, no points are awarded for a Baby Bunko, three of a kind of any number other than the mark. The turn is over and the dice are passed on to the next player.

Overs

Similar to No Babies, except that rolling three of a kind of a number other than the Mark does not end your turn, you get to keep rolling.

3-point Babies

Only 3 points are awarded for a Baby Bunko, and you get to keep rolling.

Roll-on

When the end of the game is announced at the Head Table, players rolling at all other tables, who have already rolled at least once, get to continue rolling until they fail to score. All players are entitled to the same number of turns rolling the dice. Their entire score is counted towards the final team total.

Scramble

Most fundraisers do not play with the Scramble option due to the added complexity and activity

Losers Walk

Another popular Fundraiser option, instead of having winners move up the tables, losers switch seatings. All losers move down one seating with the losers at the low table seating moving up to the high seating.

Fixed Partners

Teams play with the same partners for the entire set. New partners can be made within the pod between sets.

Bunko and Network Marketing

Network Marketing, or Multi-Level Marketing, has seen enormous growth in the last 20 years. The number of successful Network Marketing companies is on the rise, and the number of millionaires they have made continues to grow. Robert Kiyosaki of Rich-Dad, Poor-Dad fame has even said, "The BUSINESS MODEL of network marketing or multi-level marketing may be the "Perfect Business." You can get started for next to nothing and earn while you learn."

Network Marketing is not easy. Everyone has been exposed to Network Marketing as this point, whether it is AMWAY, Mary Kay, Arbonne, Pre-Paid Legal, or any one of dozens of other popular MLM businesses. They often get to the point of dreading being invited over to a "product pitch" where they feel obligated to sit through a sales discussion, feel pressured to join the program, and buy things they often are unsure they really need. If you're an old hand at this, you have probably found that many people you invite will get multiple "party" invitations a month. How will you differentiate yours?

Bunko provides a great alternative to the standard MLM party. I have had dozens of people ask about how to use Bunko as part of a Network Marketing party. I get more emails every week asking just this question. There are many ways to incorporate Bunko into your MLM party. Here I will discuss one way that I have seen work well, and some of the things to do and what NOT to do.

The Party Invitation

Start with a standard Bunko party. Using normal rules, progressive Bunko, and traveling is a good foundation for your Bunko night. Understand that you may have a little less time for game play, since you may have some novices, and you will want at least a little time to go over your product sales. Figure on having one less set than usual, or having your party run about 30 minutes longer than usual.

Invite plenty of people, ideally 20 or more. Your goal is to have at least eight people at your party, and preferably 12 or more. If you have trouble getting eight people, ask some close friends to do you a favor. Come to the party, but do not buy anything. Just help you hold a successful Bunko party. If you are already part of a Bunko group, even better. Ask members of your own Bunko Circle to come, not for the Network Marketing, but to help you keep the Bunko game running smoothly.

My advice to you is this: do NOT try to work a Network Marketing presentation into your regular Bunko Group. Some people are very turned off by this, and you will probably antagonize a few of your group members.

A second important point is this: do NOT invite people over for a Bunko party without letting them know that you will be doing some Network Marketing. You won't want them to feel tricked or ambushed. You don't have to come out and say "Hey, I'm having an [Amway/Mary Kay/Mannatech] party to get you to join my downline! However, you do not want to hide the fact either.

An invitation along the following lines works well:

It's Bunko Night at Mary's Place!

Join us for a Night of Bunko!
Fun, Food and Free Prizes

We'll be playing Bunko, March 3rd
from 7:30 to 9:30 and will be giving
away selections from the latest
[Arbonne] collection!

RSVP to Mary at 555.1212.

The Party Operation

Ok, you have your twelve guests lined up, now what are you going to do?

One of the most popular methods is to play for product. Get a small collection of samples or inexpensive products, typical hostess awards or party gifts. These will be the prizes you give out during the evening. Not only will you be giving out product, but people WANT to win it! It will also give you an excuse to tell a little about each different item you are giving away.

Play each set separately, with the awards for that set coming from your sample selection. Before each set, you have the perfect opportunity to discuss the new item you will be giving away, the benefits, and put it out on display. Then give out awards for Most Wins, and Most Bunkos at the end of the set.

Between sets is still a great time for food and drinks, with the additional benefit of being able to pull out more products as awards for the next set, and again, describe the benefits to all.

At the end of the night, you can have one additional 'big prize' for the most wins that night. The more prizes you have to give out, the more prizes you can play for.

During the game, you can work into the discussion talk about the benefits of MLM, and of joining your down-line, but remember, this is a Bunko party, and this should be a soft-sell. Remind your friends that the whole evening is tax-deductible, and that you saved enough in taxes your first year to offset your expenses. Uncle Sam PAID YOU to go into business for yourself.

Put your products prominently on display near the food area, and be ready to answer questions about them as they come up.

Typical Game-Night Timeline (7:30-9:30+ party)

- **7:30-7:45** Greetings, getting settled, basic rules
- **7:45-7:55** Short intro of the new product line and show the prizes for that set
- **7:55-8:25** Play the first six rounds
- **8:25-8:40** Award the prizes, have your main course.
- **8:40-8:50** While they finish eating, introduce next products and prizes for that set
- **8:50-9:15** Play the next six rounds
- **9:15-9:30** Award prizes, have dessert
- **9:30-???** Open invitation to stick around, place orders, discuss business options.

If you want to make the party longer, you can even add another round of play.

People have combined their Bunko party with a Theme party to add even more fun and mayhem. A slumber party style party, with an opportunity for "Makeup" sessions can combine nicely with products like Arbonne, Mary Kay, Avon and such.

Obviously, products such as Longeberger baskets can be shown in use at the party, and Pampered Chef products can be demonstrated creating the meal elements. Nutritional, health and diet products also integrate easily.

Whatever you choose to sell, it should not be too hard to find a way to make it part of your Bunko Night!

Until recently, with 7 million players, Bunko might have been the biggest little game nobody had ever heard of. Sometime around 2002, the media started to catch on that there was something going on with this game called "Bunko" that was growing like a wild fire. The culmination of this re-birth occurred in 2006, when Prilosec OTC® decided they could capitalize on this attention in an extremely bold marketing move.

Turns out, that according to their research, Bunko players had about double the incidence of heartburn as non-bunko players. Add to that the fact that 50% of women with heartburn buy remedies based on the recommendations of their friends, and the rationale for their interest becomes crystal clear.

In 2006, Prilosec OTC sponsored the first "World Bunco Championships" in Las Vegas, Nevada. Sanctioned by the World Bunco Association, they put up a very nice web site at www.BuncoCentral.com, got a celebrity involved in the person of Marg Helgenberger, made a TV deal with the Oxygen Network, and finally anteed up $50,000 so that 1000 women from all around the country could get together and roll the dice.

The event, held at the Paris Casino, was a huge success. Enough so that they contracted with the World Bunco Association, to sponsor the event until 2008, and went on to host a series of regional tournaments in Kansas City, MO, San Antonio, TX, Atlantic City, NJ and Nashville, TN. Four regional finalists and two additional players chosen by wildcard drawings won trips to the finals at the Mandalay Bay in 2007.

2007 World Championships at Mandalay Bay

The 2007 event was an even larger success. Online registration for the first 1000 players was full within 12 hours, and they soon had 2000 players waitlisted to play.

Sandra Lee was the celebrity this time, providing custom Bunko meals, and the Lifetime Channel got the TV show, producing "Let the Good Time Roll: The 2007 Bunco World Championship".

The tournament was held in three rounds, with about 400 people playing each round. The players were seated in table grouping of 12 players, just like a regular Bunko night, with a central stage that held the Head table grouping for the entire event, and from where the emcee ran the operation.

Between sets at the 2007 Bunco World Championships

The winners from the three rounds went on to play in the semifinals on the second day, until finally the top players met at a final table of four where the first player to roll a Bunko would win. Stephanie, from Scottsdale, AZ, took home the $50,000 prize.

The event took place over 2 days, with the preliminary sets held on a Saturday, and the Semifinals and finals held on Sunday.

What a Party!

Imagine, if you can, 2000 people (and about 90% women), in town for the weekend, ready to play Bunko for about 3-4 hours each day, and to enjoy the city the rest of the time! The Mandalay Bay has a great facility, and the folks at Proctor and Gamble provided giveaways, free sodas, a pay bar, and lots of entertainment, from Bunko "Cheerleaders", and an entertaining Master of Ceremonies, to the beefcake crown-bearer and round-announcer.

The Winner's Prize

Each set had a theme, just as they did in 2006. The themes for 2007 were All-American, The 50's, and Disco night. Many of the players dressed up, and prizes were awarded for best costume.

Many of the players showed up in groups, with entire Bunko circles arriving together. The seating was first come, first served, and many of these hometown Bunko circles were able to play together, knowing that one of the members of their group was going to be making it to the semifinals.

My Experience at World's

I could tell you a little about what happened between the Bunko tournament's first day play, and the semifinals, but you know what they say – "What Happens in Vegas, Stays in Vegas."

I was fortunate enough to be seated at the Head Table for the third round, with newfound friends from Alaska, Wisconsin, and California. I had traveled from Dallas, making ours quite a geographically diverse table! Luck was on my side in the beginning, and I piled up wins and Bunko's early and often. Twice I rolled a Bunko within my first two turns, with the large air-horn going off just behind my ear, announcing the end of the round. I know that ticked about 400 people off! I had three Bunkos by the fifth round.

My luck had run its course by then, and I finished the two sets with those same three Bunko bracelets, and only two wins in the last 7 games. I didn't make it to the semifinals. Not this year.

Of course, there's always 2008!

Pencil in March 7-9, 2008 for the third annual World Bunko Championship. Remember though, if you want to join me there, the event registration fills up FAST. Twelve - hours fast this year. So keep visiting BuncoCentral.com, and be ready when they open the floodgates. It looks like they will have twice the players this year. The website says 2000. Woohoo!

"If God doesn't play dice with the world, why do I always get Snake Eyes?"
Karen D. Frazer

Most of the commonly asked questions are covered in the rules above, but this is a convenient place for a quick answer, when a question does arrive.

Q: What happens in the case of a tie at the end of a round?
A: At the end of a round, a tie may occur at any of the lower tables. There are two alternatives:
Standard: Continue play until someone scores and the tie is broken.
Optional: Let everyone take a turn, team high score wins. In the case of another tie, keep playing until the tie is broken.

Q: How do you break ties at the end of the game (Most wins, for example?)
A: All players who are tied have a roll off. The Mark is 6. Each player gets one turn. At the end of the turn, the high score wins. In the case of another tie, all players that are still tied have another roll-off until the tie is finally broken.

Q: Can I count a Bunko rolled in a tiebreaker on my scoresheet?
A: Sorry, Bunkos only count during regular round play. Bunkos game tiebreakers do not count.

Q: One of my dice fell crooked. It is mostly showing the Mark. Can I count it?

A: If any dice are crooked, or fall off the rolling surface, all three dice must be re-rolled and the roll does not count.

Q: One of my dice fell crooked, but my other dice (or two dice) show the mark. I do not want to roll over; I don't care about the third die.

A: If ANY dice are crooked, or fall off the rolling surface, all three dice MUST be re-rolled and the roll does not count.

Q: How do we know when to start rolling at the lower tables?

A: The Scorekeeper at the Head Table should either (A) announce the beginning of a round, or (B) ring the table bell to indicate the beginning of a round.

Q: It was my turn to roll, and the Head Table bell rang just as I was rolling. Do I get to continue rolling?

A: If you have not rolled any dice this turn (for example you just got the dice from your right and were about to start a turn of rolling, you do NOT get to roll. Dice are considered to be rolled only if they were on the table (they may be rolling or spinning) before the bell was rang, or the end of the turn was announced.

Q: I was in the middle of rolling and the bell rang. Do I get to continue rolling?

A: If you had already rolled once and had scored at least one point in the previous roll, you get to continue rolling until you fail to score a point. (Exception: Dead Stop option – see above)

Q: My dice fell on the floor. I see a six. Can I count it?

A: If any dice are crooked, or FALL OFF the rolling surface, all three dice MUST be re-rolled and the roll does not count.

Q: Martha didn't show, and now we have only eleven players. Do we have to play with just two tables?

A: Not at all. You now have a haunted Bunko Night! Really! Their Ghost replaces the missing person. The Ghost takes a seat, and move around as if it were a regular player. Whoever has the Ghost for a partner rolls for the Ghost. If there are two Ghosts they cannot be partners, so just switch at the table.

Q: Ok, I'm partnered with a Ghost, and the Ghost rolled a Bunko! Now what?

A: There is a strategy to Bunko, having a ghost for a partner can help! The Ghost's partner is credited with any of the Ghost's Bunkos, Traveling, etc. Sometimes both sitting players want to partner with the new "Ghost" player. In this case, the players can have a roll-off to determine who gets the Ghost.

Q: How do you spell Bunko/Bunko/Bonko?

A: However makes you happy. Bunco with a 'c' is the most common variant, and is the spelling used in "Bunco squad", derived from the game of Bunco. I lean towards Bunko with a 'k'. However, feel free to take a crayon and change every 'k' to a 'c' in this document. (Just don't press too hard on the screen if you are reading this at your computer.)

Q: Why didn't you mention our version? We score to 50 points by twos and after scoring a Bunko have to jump around the room in a counter-clockwise circle, on one foot, while singing Waltzing Matilda?

A: There are so many variations of the game, I am certain I have missed some of the classic versions. I'm sorry. I really would love to hear the details of your version. Please head on over to www.BunkoBook.com and join our discussion boards and bulletin boards where you can list your particular flavor. Alternatively, email me at ask@BunkoBook.com

Q: This Bunco World Championship sounds cool! Where can I find out more?

A: Go to www.BuncoCentral.com to find out more. For a list of useful Bunko websites, just check at the end of this book, or find a page of links at this books web page:

www.BunkoBook.com

Appendix B: Sample Game Rules

If you have read this far, you must realize the Rules of Bunko are varied with lots of personal options.

The following abbreviated rules of EZ-Bunko, and Progressive Bunko can be freely used. For lots more rules that your group can use and make their own, visit http://www.BunkoBook.com

EZ-Bunko

Rule 1: Score Points by Rolling Three Dice

The object of the game of EZ-Bunko is to win rounds of play by out scoring your opponents. A player scores by rolling sixes (the Mark) on any of their three dice when thrown. Players may also score by rolling three of a kind of any other number. A player continues rolling as long as they score one or more points. Point scoring is as follows:

  ⚅⬚⬚ 1 die showing a six = 1 point.
  ⚅⚅⬚ 2 dice (or doubles) showing sixes = 2 points
  ⚅⚅⚅ 3 dice showing sixes = 21 points
  ⚀⚀⚀ 3 of a kind dice of any other number = 5 points

Rule 2: Legal Rolls

In order for a roll to count, the dice must be lifted off the table, shaken and rolled onto the table. Dice scores count only if the dice land cleanly. If the dice land stacked or cocked all three dice are re-rolled. If any of the dice fall on the floor, all three dice are re-rolled. If one or more dice fall off the table twice during any one players turn, that ends their turn.

Rule 3: Ranking Tables and Teams

One table is designated the Head Table and controls the pace of play. The other tables are assigned an arbitrary order from lowest to highest.

Rule 4: Initial Setup

Players roll 3 dice for initial table selection. The highest four rolls sit at the Head Table, the next four at the Middle Table, and so on. Players choose their seat at random initially. Dice are rolled at each table to determine who rolls first.

Rule 5: Keeping Score

The rolling player's partner is the scorekeeper and is tasked with keeping incremental score on scratch paper. There is no specific manner in which this scoring should be kept. Scorekeepers may use scratch paper, or at the discretion of the group, mechanical counters, or any other device they may deem appropriate. At the end of each player's roll, the scorekeeper adds the player's score to the running total for their team, and announces the new team score. Any player who rolls a Bunko should mark the result on her personal scorecard.

Rule 6: Playing the Round

At the start of each round, the last player to roll from the team remaining at the table from the previous round starts the next round. The round begins with a signal from the Head Table by ringing the bell, and the players at each table begin the rolling. A round is completed when one of the teams at the Head Table scores at least 21 points. The current scorekeeper announces the end of the round again by ringing the bell, and the turns end at all tables. No score is allowed if the dice have not touched the table when the end of the round has been called, with the exception that all players are entitled to roll at least once.

Rule 7: Tracking Wins and Losses

When either team at the Head Table scores 21 they have won the round. At the lower tables, whichever team has the most points when the rolling is ended, wins the round. If there is a tie at one of the lower tables, play continues as normal until one of the teams score and break the tie. After all rolling has been completed, each player from the winning team should tally a win on her personal scorecard for that round. Each player from the losing team should tally a loss on her personal scorecard. Tallies may be marked any way as is deemed appropriate.

Rule 8: Advancing Tables

When all scores have been updated, players change places and teams. Players from the winning team at the lower tables advance one table rank towards the Head Table. The losing players at all the lower tables remain at their table, one of them switching seats. The losers from the Head table move to the lowest table. No one should play with the same partner twice in a row.

Rule 9: End of the Game

The players should decide ahead of time when the game will end. This may be at a selected number of Sets (3 or 4 is common) or at a predetermined time. When the game is over, players compute their total wins, losses and Bunkos, and prizes are awarded based on overall results.

Rule 10: Distributing Prizes

At the end of the night, any ties between players for prizes are determined by individual roll offs. Each player in the tie gets a turn rolling for a six, and accumulates points until they fail to score (as in regular play). The player with the highest score wins the tiebreaker. Players continue taking turns rolling until there is no longer a tie. Players may win more than one prize.

Progressive Bunko

Rule 1: Score Points by Rolling Three Dice

The object of the game of Bunko is to win rounds of play by out scoring your opponents. Players score by rolling three dice and matching the current number or Mark, which has been set for that round. Players take turns rolling the dice. A player continues rolling as long as they score one or more points per throw. Point scoring is as follows (example is for Round 2, making the Mark 2):

    ⬚⬚⬚ 1 die showing the Mark = 1 point.

    ⬚⬚⬚ 2 dice (or doubles) showing the Mark = 2 points

    ⬚⬚⬚ 3 dice showing the current Mark = 21 points

    ⬚⬚⬚ 3 of a kind of any other number = 5 points

Rule 2: Legal Rolls

The dice must be lifted clear, shaken and rolled on the table. Dice scores count only if the dice land cleanly. If the dice land stacked or cocked all three dice are re-rolled. If any of the dice fall on the floor, all three dice are re-rolled. If the dice fall off the table twice during one player's turn, that ends their turn.

Rule 3: Ranking Tables and Teams

One table is designated the Head Table. The Head Table controls the pace of play. The other tables are assigned an arbitrary order from lowest to highest.

Rule 4: Initial Setup

Players roll 3 dice for initial table selection. The highest four rolls sit at the Head Table, the next four second table, and so on. Players choose their seat at random. Dice are rolled to determine who rolls first.

Rule 5: Keeping Score

The rolling player's partner is the scorekeeper and is tasked with keeping score. There is no specific manner in which this scoring should be kept. At the end of each players roll, the scorekeeper adds the player's score to the running total for their team, and announces the new score. Any player who rolls a Bunko should mark the result on her personal scorecard.

Rule 6: Establishing the Mark

Bunko is played in Sets of 6 rounds. The Mark for each round is established at the start of the round, and is announced by the Head Table's scorekeeper. The Mark starts at 1 and advances by 1 up to 6, matching the number of the round within the set. Announcing the Mark is a courtesy and no penalty is incurred if the scorekeeper fails to announce the Mark.

Rule 7: "Traveling"

Bunko is played with a token called the "Traveler". When a player rolls a Bunko the current keeper of the Traveler tosses it to whoever rolled the Bunko.

At the end of game play, the person who has the Traveler wins a separate prize. Any rolling of a Bunko, except in a roll-off, is valid for exchange of the Traveler.

Rule 8: Playing the Round

At the start of each round, players roll to go first. The round begins with a signal from the scorekeeper at the Head Table, usually by ringing the bell, and the players at each table begin the rolling. A round is completed when one of the teams at the Head Table scores 21 or more points. The current scorekeeper announces the end of the round again by ringing the bell, and the turns end at all tables. No points are scored if the dice have not touched the table when the end of the round has been called, with the exception that all players are entitled to roll at least once.

Rule 9: Tracking Wins and Losses

When either team at the Head Table scores 21 they have won the round. At the lower tables, whichever team has the most points when the rolling is ended, wins the round. If there is a tie at one of the lower tables, play continues as normal until one of the teams score and break the tie. After all rolling has been completed, each player from the winning team should tally a win on her score-card for that round. Players from the losing team should tally a loss on their scorecard. Tallies may be marked any way deemed appropriate.

Rule 10: Advancing Tables

When all scores have been updated, players change places and teams. Players from the winning team at the lower tables advance one table rank towards the Head Table. The losing players at all the lower tables remain at their table, the last person to roll at the table switching seats with an open one. The losers from the Head table move to the lowest table. No one should play with the same partner twice in a row.

Rule 11: End of the Game

The players should decide ahead of time when the game will end. This may be at a selected number of Sets (3 or 4 is common) or at a predetermined time. When the game is over, players compute their total wins, losses and Bunkos, and prizes are awarded based on overall results.

Rule 12: Distributing Prizes

At the end of the night, any ties between players for prizes are determined by individual roll offs. Each player in the tie gets a turn rolling for a six, and accumulates points until they fail to score (as in regular play). The player with the highest score wins the tiebreaker. Players continue taking turns rolling until there is no longer a tie. Players may win more than 1 prize.

When playing for cash, there are many ways to divide the winnings. Here are my favorite six payoffs.

Based on $5 Kitty fee	Winners & Losers	Everyone Wins	Travelers Delight	High Payout	Straight Bunko	Bunkos Rule
Most Bunkos	20	15	20	30	20	15
Most Wins	15	10	15	20	15	10
Most Losses	10	5	10	10	10	5
Traveling	5	5	10			10
Wipeout	5	5	5			5
2nd Most Wins		5			5	
Losses=Wins		5			5	
First Bunko		5				10
Consolation	5	5			5	5

For Prize Play, here are some suggested Prize categories. Use what you like and ignore the rest! These are presented in typical order of value.

Game Prizes

Bunko Prize

For the most Bunkos

"I'm a Winner" Prize

For the most wins

Traveling Prize

For the player who rolled the last Bunko

Mediocrity Prize

For an equal number of wins and losses

Consolation Prize

For the most losses

Random Prize

Selected at Random from those who didn't win a prize

Event Prizes

Miss Charity Prize

For whoever raises the most for your favorite charity

Birthday Prize

For the player or players who have a birthday that month

Theme-stress Prize

For the player with the best theme outfit

"You Go, Girl" Prize

For the player who had the best "win" in her personal life - lost the most pounds, got off chemo, had a baby, etc.

Appendix D: Sample Game Aids

The game aids on the following pages may be freely copied for personal use.

These include Scoresheets, Roster, Cheat-Sheet, invitations, and more. For a larger selection of free Bunko materials you can use, visit www.BunkoBook.com.

High Table	Middle Table
Winners Stay, Losers stray	Winners move up, Losers stay put
Low Table	**Prize Table**
Winners move on, Losers sit 'n' yarn	**Prize Table**

's BUNKO Scoresheet for _____ / / /

Round 1 Point Tally		Pts	W/L	B
⚅				
⚄				
⚃				
⚂				
⚁				
⚀				
Totals :				

Round 2 Point Tally		Pts	W/L	B
⚅				
⚄				
⚃				
⚂				
⚁				
⚀				
Totals :				

Total Points	Wins	Losses	Buncos

BUNKO
Scorecard

NAME: _____

Bunkos	Wins	Losses

BUNKO
Scorecard

NAME: _____

Bunkos	Wins	Losses

EN-BUNKO
Scorecard

NAME: _____

Bunkos ____ Wins ____ Losses ____

1	1	1	1
2	2	2	2
3	3	3	3
4	4	4	4
5	5	5	5
6	6	6	6

EN-BUNKO
Scorecard

NAME: _____

Bunkos ____ Wins ____ Losses ____

1	1	1	1
2	2	2	2
3	3	3	3
4	4	4	4
5	5	5	5
6	6	6	6

BUNKO Group

Date	Hostess	Address	Phone	Food	Food 2	Food 3

SUBS

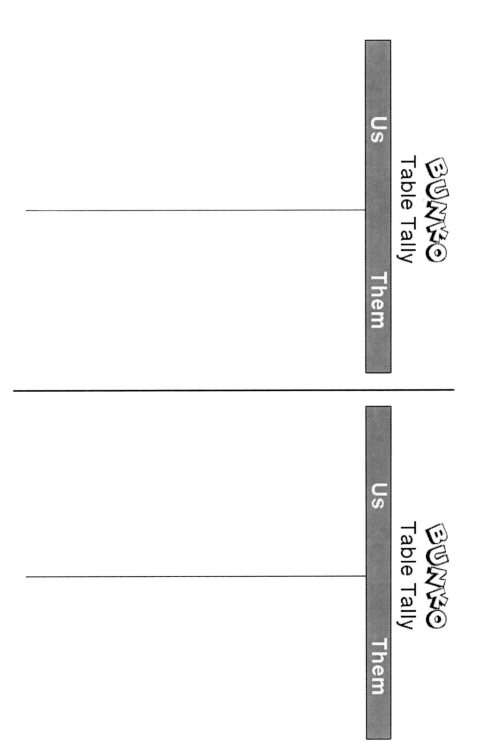

LET'S PLAY BUNKO!

We are starting a BUNKO NIGHT for the neighborhood. BUNKO is a dice game that is easy to play. No experience needed.

Expect lots of FUN and LAUGHS.

It's a great opportunity to get to know your neighbors!

When:
Where:
     Call:

Bunko Newbie Cheat-Sheet

Rules for Table #1

The number of the round is the point to be played for (the **MARK**)

First team to score 21 points wins.

Players earn points by rolling 3 dice.

One MARK scores 1 point.

Two MARKS scores two points.

Three MARKS scores 21 points.

Three of any other number scores five points.

Scoring

Target number = 1 ⚀

⚀ ⚁ ⚂ = 1 point

⚀ ⚄ ⚀ = 2 points

⚀ ⚀ ⚀ = 21 points = Bunko!

⚅ ⚅ ⚅ = 5 points

(3 of a kind NOT the Mark)

21 points at High Table wins

Highest scores at other tables win

Continue to roll the dice as long as you are scoring. When you fail to score pass the dice to your left.

Play at the Lower Tables (#2 and 3)

All play begins when Table #1 announces the MARK and continues until Table #1 announces a win, which stops all play at all tables. The high team score at each table wins the round. Points are scored during play the same as at Table #1.

If three MARKS (a Bunko), are scored, continue the play. Scores sometimes are very high, often over 50.

No score is allowed if the dice have not **touched the table** when the game is called.

All players are allowed at least one turn.

In case of a tie, one turn around for each player will decide the winning team.

End of the Round

Wins and losses are marked on each player's card. No wins will be scored once a player leaves the table.

At the end of each round the winning team from the Middle and Low tables move up to a higher table. The losing team from the High table moves to the low table. During the switch, partners are changed.

Visit us at www.BunkoBook.com and download Rosters, Scoresheets, Rules Sets, Table Tallies and more!

Other Favorite Websites of *The Bunko Book*:

- **www.BuncoCentral.com** – Home of the World Bunko Championships
- **www.BuncoRules.com** – How can I resist – the original Bunko survey!
- **www.eBunco.com** – Bunko Shopping
- **www.Bunco.com** – More Bunko shopping, home of The Bunco® Dice Game
- **www.worldbunco.com** – Home of the World Bunco Association, rules, newsletters and more
- **www.DiceGamers.com** – Lots of Dice game stuff, especially Bunko
- **www.buncogameshop.com** – Lots more Bunko shopping
- **bunco.kewlbox.com** – BuncoCentral sponsored online Bunko play!
- **www.mediafiends.com** – Home to Patti's Pair-a-dice. The best Bunko theme site on the web. Find it in the Forums.
- **www.rc3group.com** – The original Dice with Spice Cookbook

Steven Pratt sells and supports networking software at his day job. By night, he toils away as the webmaster of www.BuncoRules.com and www.FrumperSticker.com as well as working on numerous different side-projects at any one time.

He lives in the suburbs of Dallas, with his wife Tricia, daughter Jensen, and Sunny, their Australian Cattledog.

You can email him at Steve@TheBunkoBook.com

NOTES:

Printed in the United States
110441LV00001B/131/A

9 780979 836206